CIVIL ENDOWMENT

Published by:
Rinchen Publications
20 John St.
Kingston, NY 12401

www.rinchen.com

First Edition; September, 2015
ISBN 978-0-9714554-7-4

COVER & INTERIOR DESIGN: T. Reitzle
EDITOR: Arya-francesca Jenkins

IMAGE CREDITS
AUTHOR PHOTO: Robert Hansen-Sturm
COVER IMAGE: perets/iStock
PAGES 84-85: Lisa Berry/Wish Media
PAGE 119: Michael Erlewine
PAGE 120: Blacqbook/Dollar Photo Club
PAGE 123: FreeImages.com/Issachar Brooks

CIVIL ENDOWMENT

The Transformation
of Economic Power

David N. McCarthy

RINCHEN

Contents

This book is dedicated to the UNIVERSAL BENEFICIARY: *all human beings now living and those yet to be born.*

CHAPTER ONE

What is Civil Endowment?

T HE CIVIL ENDOWMENT SYSTEM THAT IS PROPOSED IN THIS
book is a structural innovation for the contemporary world
economy. It is not something that currently exists. There are some
trends and movements that share certain similar characteristics
and goals, but the substance of what is being described here has
no precedent. Although it is an innovation, it has been designed
to take its place in our existing economy in harmony with what is
already here. Rather than tearing down the old economy, it seeks
to transform it.

Why do we need structural innovation? If we look at the history
of the modern economy, starting with the Industrial Revolution, it
would be absurd to think that everything has proceeded perfectly,
and that no adjustments or improvements need to be made. In fact,
it might be easier for many to believe that the modern economy
is an unmitigated disaster. As if looming ecological catastrophe
were not enough, issues of economic injustice and wealth inequality have only become more glaring over time, not less. As well,
extreme poverty lingers—with no real end in sight—as a blight on
the whole human family.

Others may be quick to point out that the modern economy has created tremendous prosperity and wellbeing for countless people. Isn't it so that there is truth in both views? In any case, the historical process of modernity is more or less irreversible. Maybe a tiny percentage of us could go back to a very low-tech, agrarian, or hunter-gatherer economy. But if you think about it realistically, the way forward is toward a society that uses technology in clean and skillful ways, while reversing the errors of the primitive technological age—an age from which we must emerge.

For those who have been seriously considering the predicaments of our times, the real question is not about the need for structural innovation in the economy. It is more like, "What sort of innovation would really make a difference?" Along with that is the question of whether such innovation is practically feasible. Any proposal worth talking about needs to fulfill both these criteria: It must be a genuine structural improvement, and it must be possible. I would like to assert from the beginning that the proposed civil endowment system meets these conditions.

What follows is a basic description of civil endowment. Although it is tempting to provide a preamble with all the considerations and supportive reasoning that have gone into its development, we will leave that for later chapters. First, let us consider the essence of what is being proposed.

The fundamental idea of civil endowment is to establish and maintain bodies of capital to be invested for the benefit of the whole of humanity, on an unbounded time horizon. What is meant by the "whole of humanity" is: all human beings now living, and all those yet to be born. This grouping is called the universal beneficiary. An "unbounded time horizon" means, in simplest terms, "as far forward as we can imagine or foresee." These two main characteristics are intimately connected since, if we are talking about all human beings yet to be born, we are inevitably talking about an unbounded time horizon.

The invested wealth that will make up civil endowments can simply be called civil capital. Civil capital is capital of which the beneficial owner is the universal beneficiary. Establishing the idea of the universal beneficiary is a way of formalizing and pointing out the conception of the human whole (all present and future human beings) in our capacity as recipients of the benefits of this system of investments. The very nature of the universal beneficiary requires a very specific approach to investment practice, one that would promote long-term environmental and social wellbeing, as well as universal opportunity and economic justice. The practical thinking about how such investments would be undertaken can be called simply a civil investment protocol, which could evolve over time into a body of knowledge, a portfolio theory of civil endowment.

Civil Capital is definitely *economic capital.*

Civil capital is definitely economic capital in the most fundamental sense of the term. It is not abstract capital such as "social capital" or "human capital;" nor is it "natural capital." It is a portion of the productive economy that is endowed to the human whole. Practically speaking, it would involve any and all sorts of investments that private or institutional investors make in today's world. This would include direct ownership stakes in new or existing businesses, land and real estate of all kinds and, as well, investment in the financial instruments and securities that constitute the indirect ownership characteristic of the contemporary financial world. As a civil endowment system emerges at significant scale, this will create nothing less than a "civil sector" of the productive economy. As this sector evolves, new types of businesses, financial institutions, and financial instruments will emerge with it.

Civil capital is by no means meant to replace private property or the private sector generally. It is actually part of the private sector, in the sense that it is distinguished from state ownership or control. What civil endowment *is* meant to do is create a *qualitative stimulus* of a particular kind for the global economy. This stimulus is intended to be one that is fundamentally transformative. The particular nature of that transformation—which is in the direction that a conscious, compassionate person today understands we need to go—will be in the direction of environmental and social sustainability, along with providing a realistic prospect for universal economic opportunity and justice. The productivity of civil capital can provide a great deal of needed direct assistance to humanity's poorest members, along with many other dimensions of benefit and wellbeing for people generally.

The Transformation of Economic Power

As we will see, civil capital can be understood as a reformation of capital at a very basic level. It can even be seen as the completion or perfection of the capital concept. As a theoretical insight, that would perhaps not be all that important, if it were not for the fact that the manifestation of capital in action is in fact the exercise of economic power. That being so, then the changes that caring people know must happen can be brought about by changes in how this power is applied.

How is it that we manifest economic power through capital? The answer is simply that capital is at the root of productivity in several ways: it enables productivity; it reproduces and maintains productivity; and it structures productivity. We will examine all these aspects of economic power, the key point here being that the governing spirit of civil capital is to do all these things for the common good of all humanity. As we will see, the initial source of that transformation is unbiased compassion put into action through the practice of generosity.

The Provenance of Civil Capital

The French have a wry saying, "If my aunt had wheels, she'd be a bicycle." That is the sort of reaction that might easily come up for a world-wise person in regard to this idea. It is easy to think, "Well, fine; it would be great if there were these bodies of capital invested for the common good. But how will they be created?"

Perhaps the single, most critical psychological leap involved with believing this is really a feasible idea is coming to the realization that *human generosity is equal to the task.* In short, civil endowments can be gifted to the whole of humanity by individuals acting independently and as part of organizations.

There are several important points that will make this premise easier to accept. The first of these is the matter of scale. As I contemplated this idea, I realized that the creation of aggregations of resource to be permanently endowed to the human whole is *positive and significant on any scale.* Although it is true that to have any tangible effect, the sums involved would have to be large enough to be actually invested in some way, they would not have to be large in per capita terms.

There are several reasons for this. First, the act of giving is transformative to the giver. Just to give any amount for such a purpose creates a kind of connection and intention toward the healing, abundance, and unity of the human family. It gives a sense of participation in a vision that is incredibly positive and hopeful. As well, the existence of civil endowments, however small, will inspire others. At the beginning, what is really needed is the dissemination of the awareness of the very existence of such an idea. It is also far more likely that people will take this seriously if an example of it—however small—exists, rather than it just being an idea or proposal. Therefore, we should understand that there is a symbolic level in the formation and development of civil endowments. For that level, it is fine to start small.

The second key point about generosity is that the main way that really significant resources would eventually be brought into the system will be through what can be called "structuralized generosity." This could take place in various ways. Many businesses and institutions today donate a small portion of their cash flow to various causes. It has also long been proposed to collect various kinds of small fees on cash flows for things like currency exchanges, money transfers, sales of securities, and the like. Maynard Keynes (himself a speculator in financial markets) proposed that small fees be imposed on stock and bond transactions as a disincentive to speculation. Nobel Laureate economist James Tobin proposed micro-taxes on currency exchanges with a similar motivation, and to fund worthy causes. The idea of creating such flows into civil endowment would not be to impose taxes through government, but instead to motivate enterprises sympathetic to the system to donate a very low percentage as an overhead deduction from transactions.

This possibility becomes even more believable when you realize that civil endowments will be capitalizing operational businesses. Returning micro-percentage flows of funds from their transaction stream could easily be instituted as part of the spirit of participation in the movement. There are, in fact, many avenues of generosity that could develop. The primary question is not so much whether human beings are generous enough. It is more a question of demonstrating to people how civil endowment is a worthy object of their generosity.

Although it is important to see that generosity is in and of itself sufficient in creating and maintaining civil capital, it is also likely that, over time, a primary source of its growth will be the productivity of the capital itself.

The Institutional Basis

The proposed organizational structure for civil endowments will be put forth in detail in the chapter called "The Special Proposal." Here, we will take a preliminary look at the main features of the system. The first main point is that civil endowments would be managed by civil society organizations, not government or business entities. Second, this would be a decentralized system. The civil endowment model is a meme that can be replicated in any number of variations and locations.

The key point in the methodology of civil investment is that decisions would be subject to the "foundational spirit" of civil capital. This particular point will be discussed in much greater detail in the ensuing chapters where we look into the very essence and nature of capital. A central insight that emerges is that capital is essentially a creation of the human mind, which is then set to work in the tangible manifestations of the economy. If the human mind, working both socially and individually, creates capital, we can restructure or reform capital in the direction of the common good. This sort of thinking is behind a catch phrase that conveys a lot in a few words: "Capitalism can't be reformed, but capital can."

Another essential point in the implementation of civil capital is accountability, especially to civil society. Promoting accountability and openness in organizations is always going to be a challenge. However, by the very nature of its commitment to the universal beneficiary, the organizations behind civil investment will have— inherently at least—nothing to hide, no divisive agenda, and no one to exclude.

Concerning the possible types of administrative structures for endowments, I have identified three main categories, namely, platonic, democratic, and commons-style.

The platonic form of administration is similar to what we have in today's world of pension funds, wealth management practices, and endowments for institutions such as universities. In those arenas, the actual investment decisions are made by trained professionals, under the direction of the owners of the assets. There are trillions of dollars in assets managed in this way in today's world.

Capitalism can't be reformed, but capital can.

With a democratic form of administration, there are several possible levels of stakeholder involvement. Even in a platonic style of governance, some decisions might logically be made by vote, for example. As for a more broad-based democracy, such as having elected representatives, I do not envision a workable way for this to happen, at least not initially.

This possibility will be explored in more depth in future chapters and it should certainly be understood as a long-term prospect or goal of such a system. Initially though, it seems that the best way to ensure accountability to the goals of civil endowment (and to civil society generally) is to have decisions made by specially trained and qualified individuals, working in teams that practice mutual accountability. The accountability of decision makers would be structured into the endowment organizations themselves and then, at a second level, monitored and enforced by a separate certifying agency. As well, by virtue of those decisions being made openly, there would be oversight by, and accountability to, civil society generally. It goes without saying that civil investments would also be subject to legal oversight and, inevitably, to the reasonable conventions of business.

Commons-style governance offers some very bright prospects in regard to civil endowment, although this area of practice and discourse is not very well understood in society today. The commons has deep historical roots, but it is a way of thinking and acting that has been submerged and marginalized in our shared imagination of society and economic life. The commons is directly associated with civil society, since it is a realm of economic practice that is fundamentally different than either political governance or private property. It is possible that a civil endowment, or a system of endowments, could be understood and administered as a commons, but this is not something we can simply assume or declare to be the case.

A basic point about a commons is that it is created and maintained through conscious social agreements and rules. If the necessary level of consciousness and agreement were to emerge in society, civil endowments could come to be established as a "capital commons." Although the "commons way of thinking" would seem to be a wonderful prospect in regard to civil endowment governance, we need to regard it as a provisional prospect, simply because the application of these ideas to capital management is an entirely untested concept. Awareness of the importance of commons-style resource management is growing rapidly, and it is an immensely interesting and promising trend. Still, I believe that civil endowments will be initially established with a platonic administrative model, which could then evolve in a conscious transition to broader commons-based and democratic styles of governance.

It is possible that this introductory description of the civil endowment idea brings up as many questions as it answers. Ensuing chapters will explore all these main points in greater detail.

In summary, civil endowment is a proposed structural innovation for the world economy, which is intended to be a feasible, realistic, and incremental program to remedy the glaring defects of the environmentally destructive and socially toxic system we have today. The key point of the proposal is to create a system of civil capital endowments that will remain in permanent trust for the common good of humanity. The intent of these endowments will be to provide a qualitative stimulus to transform the economy in the direction of environmental regeneration, universal sufficiency and opportunity, and justice.

CHAPTER TWO

The Foundations
of the Vision

I T IS ABUNDANTLY CLEAR THAT THE HUMAN PREDICAMENT OF our time demands a fresh approach to economics. Since economics emerged in the 19th century as a separate discipline, there has been a massive expansion of knowledge and cultural resources available for its use. The very landscape of views and ideas has evolved to include the richness of the intellectual legacy of the entire world. Despite this fact, most of what guides conventional thinking in economics to this day is derived from 18th century, European scientific thought—particularly the view of an objective external universal operating according to mechanistic laws. Countervailing leftist theory draws largely on 19th century utopian and revolutionary views.

By contrast, contemporary strains of economic thought can now draw on a radically expanded base of intellectual resources. For example, authentic presentations of the philosophies of the East are now widely available, such as those found in Buddhism, Hinduism, and Taoism. The same is true for new disciplines that have emerged in the West, such as Environmental Science, Systems Theory, and profound scientific ideas such as Relativity and the Uncertainty Principle.

We also have the lessons of recent history to draw upon. For example, although state socialism may have seemed like a good idea to many a century or so ago, there is now a body of practical evidence that points conclusively to its shortcomings. More recently, the accelerating wealth divide and the corrosive effects of business interests on politics and the environment all point to fundamental deficiencies in so-called free-market capitalism. It is no longer a valid argument to put forth laissez-faire thinking in response to the defects of socialism. Perhaps less obviously, it is equally time-worn thinking to propose government intervention as the only remedy for the shortcomings of modern capitalism.

Both state socialism and corporate capitalism are fundamentally flawed.

Since roughly the mid-20th century, there have been many fine examples of creative thinking in the field that transcend the strictures of orthodox theory, both through the use of expanded conceptual toolsets, and through simple observation and intellectual honesty. The pioneering efforts of Kenneth Boulding, E.F. Schumacher, Hazel Henderson, and Herman Daly come to mind in this regard. Their work was foundational for the movement now called "The New Economics." Though the views of these and other progressive economic thinkers are studied and respected in certain circles, their ideas have remained largely outside the mainstream of academia, the media, the business world—and especially politics.

It is probably true that an approach to economics that puts human and environmental values first will never become a dominant point of view through the evolution of theory alone. Fortunately, however, there is also a lot of cultural pressure to move in the direction of environmental sustainability and greater economic justice—even as the forces of reaction against these ideals seem ever more powerful and brazen.

Since theory alone will not produce the changes we need, it follows that the course of action *that does have* a prospect of success would be a decisive movement toward tangible implementation of a new, saner brand of economic thinking—one that actually accords with our current reality. I believe a civil endowment system, as described in *The Special Proposal*, is such a prospect.

Civil endowment theory evolved out of years of careful study of the pioneers of New Economics, and from my own experience working in the sustainability movement. It was refined by an extended study of the history of economic reasoning, and of capital theory in particular. Most fundamentally, the root of the theory rests on a Buddhist understanding of the world. That said, this is not an attempt at a systematic presentation of "Buddhist economics," nor is it intended to be a specifically Buddhist proposal. It is meant to be understood by anyone, and to be universally applicable in practice in our present-day world.

The principle of interdependence is one of the hallmarks of Buddhist teachings, and it provides a guiding systemic principle for everything that follows. At the social level, the principle of compassion provides a background of attitude and motivation. Civil endowment theory has much to recommend it in a purely theoretical realm of economic thought, but I suggest that it can only succeed in practice as an economics of compassion.

Chapter Three presents an outline of how we might think generally about an economics of compassion from a Buddhist point of view. Although there certainly could be other philosophical ways to construct an economics of compassion, it is essential that we think about at least one such backdrop of guiding principles. As will hopefully be clear, the structure of the civil endowment theory is such that it cannot be presented or proposed merely as a financial technology. Arguably, it would work—at least to some degree—if implemented without the inner guiding spirit of compassion. But the catch is that, without such a spirit, people would be very unlikely to do the work to implement it in the first place. In essence, the motivating power for this work is concern for the wellbeing of all of us going forward. Just as anger and resentment are the bases of some revolutions, the revolution I propose is based on kindness and compassion.

Although these ideas arose most fundamentally out of a search for an economics of compassion for our time, the practical matters involved have always come back to the question of causality. If systems function—and indeed come into being—out of a matrix of causal processes, then how can we work with and structure those processes to move the economy in the direction in which it clearly must move?

We should remain mindful here that the crises of our times are absolutely fundamental. They involve the very survival of the human race—or certainly of civilization in any desirable sense of the word. For example, if you simply think about the issue of sea-level rise due to projected ice melt from climate change, and look at maps of what the world could easily look like in coming centuries, you know that humanity is going to be in for a tough ride. In particular, we need to solve the problem of the macro-scale burning of fossil fuels on the most urgent conceivable basis. Our current economic and political systems are inadequate to this task. Although there is currently a great deal of welcome progress in the area of renewable energy, this book is being written at a time when climate deniers hold a majority in both houses of the United States Congress. And climate change is not the only problem we face. Although political reforms are going to have to be part of the solution, the unfortunate reality is that even very mild, reasonable, and fair legislative or regulatory proposals and policies face huge (and sadly, effective) obstructionism. As much as we should honor and support political activism, and view it as necessary, we cannot pin our hopes on it. It stands too great a chance of being ineffective. It is too slow, too clumsy, and inconclusive. Political leadership in our times mirrors the deep ideological rifts in our society and is therefore profoundly divided. That being so, it is far more likely that effective political leadership and change will arise out of economic innovation, rather than the reverse. Although it might seem unlikely, I believe there is a way forward through civil-society economic activism that will magnetize the forces of the public and the business world and bring political leadership into line with it. Given the wide range of civil society-based initiatives and movements that are afoot in the world today, it is not particularly farfetched to think that we can create a new one.

There is a way forward through civil-society economic activism.

The idea of creating an investment process for the common good arose out of a perception of what is needed, and in particular how to achieve certain results. It did not come about from economic theory *per se*. The contemplation of capital theory, which we'll examine in depth in chapters five and six, came after the idea of civil capital had become fairly clear to me. The intellectual analysis, however, provides a very solid foundation and justification for civil capital, which is needed if this body of thought is to be communicated effectively, and take its place in the realm of economic reasoning.

It is not important whether you come to an understanding of the potential value of civil capital somewhat intuitively, as I initially did, or through a more elaborate thought process grounded in economic analysis. In any case, a focus on the ongoing process of investment is very important, because to understand it is to actually see the way that the economy is continually reinventing, renewing, and potentially reforming itself. Investment is like a meridian point in Chinese medicine, or an articulation point that enables movement in a structure. It is a place where change can happen, and not just new iterations of existing patterns. It is a place where innovation can happen.

This understanding, of course, is what is behind the socially responsible investing (SRI) movement. For the purpose of simplicity in this discussion, I am grouping Impact Investing with SRI, although they are not identical. For all the good intentions and innovation that the SRI movement embodies, at least as it is currently practiced, it really has no hope of providing universal sufficiency, universal opportunity, and the scale of qualitative transformation needed at this time. Something more radical is needed.

To be clear, I'm not a critic of socially responsible investing. In fact, I'm a big admirer. I believe it has laid the foundation for the investment practices that are necessary for civil endowments. It is just that it is not sufficient to the task.

It is important to differentiate between civil endowment and SRI. Let's take a quick look at how they differ. The most obvious and significant of these ways is that the private individuals who make socially responsible investments retain ownership of the investments themselves, and receive any profits that arise from them. SRI is a movement that works within the existing capitalist system without challenging or changing the fundamental way that capital operates in society. As such, it is both successful and beneficial. Unfortunately, SRI in and of itself will not solve the problems and crises that humanity faces in the present and immediate future. It is inadequate both in terms of structure and scale. Admittedly, this is a statement of opinion.[1] Although the social and environmental effects of SRI are intended to benefit everyone (and certainly do), the economic outcome of the movement has had little impact on the wealth divide, the behavior of most of the really big corporations, or the world-destroying juggernaut of fossil fuel extraction and consumption. It is a start, but it cannot finish the job. SRI is a type of private investment. It reflects the admirable intentions of people who invest in that way. But let's be clear that such investments ultimately benefit them in terms of profit and ownership.

The key difference between a private investment of any kind and a civil endowment lies in its ownership. In the case of civil endowment, the beneficial owner of the assets and their productivity is the universal beneficiary. (Hereafter this term will sometimes be abbreviated as "UB.") The leap that takes civil capital beyond any sort of private investment is the provisioning of the productivity and profit of such capital, as well as its ultimate ownership, to the common good.

---

1) For a rather pessimistic endorsement of this view, see *Green Capitalism, the God that Failed* by Richard Smith (WEA Books 2015).

BENEFICIAL OWNER is a term used to designate the party for whom the economic benefits of an asset—its profit or productivity and the ownership of the asset itself—are assigned. The term is used in a FIDUCIARY RELATIONSHIP, i.e., one in which a party manages assets for another party. This is most commonly the case, for example, in the case of trust funds, or the management of financial portfolios or pension funds.

Practically speaking, what makes it possible to assign an asset to an abstract entity like the universal beneficiary—and to undertake to manage it on behalf of the universal beneficiary—is the existence of a fiduciary organization as its administrator. Clearly, such capital needs to be managed by a fiduciary organization, since the UB is the whole of the human race, including people not yet born.

Before we explore the details and ramifications of how all this could work, let's take an in-depth look at the ultimate basis of civil endowment: the economics of compassion.

CHAPTER THREE

The Economics of Compassion

T HE POSSIBILITY OF ASSOCIATING ECONOMICS AND COMPASSION in some sort of rigorous way might seem rather improbable at this point in history. Both the established theory of the discipline and the events that play out on the world stage incline us, if not to outright despair, certainly to worry. Profound pessimism over the human prospect often seems like the most realistic attitude. Economics, we will remember, is called "the dismal science," and not without reason.

Nevertheless, I invite you to give this somewhat improbable juxtaposition a fair chance. We will look at the idea of an economics of compassion in terms of two basic questions. First, how would a general outlook of compassion inform our thinking and actions in the realm of economics? And second, if we do adopt such an outlook in theory and practice, are the outcomes actually economical? In other words, are there economies of compassion, just as there are economies of scale?

The two parts of the first question correspond to the theoretical and practical sides of economics. Can we derive theoretical insights about economics using compassion as a guiding principle? And what sorts of tangible actions might we take, starting at the individual level and going all the way to the structure of our most fundamental institutions?

The question about economies of compassion will be taken up throughout this chapter and in more detail in the next chapter on economic wisdom. Suffice to say here that there are indeed very positive economies of compassion, a fact that will become more and more obvious as we go along.

Even if it is something of a stretch, it would be hard for a decent person to disagree, at least in principle, with the idea that if compassion could provide a guiding principle in economics it would be a good thing. However, because the subjects seem quite far apart, it may be helpful to start with a less controversial idea: that economic theory and practice ought to be based on wisdom. If wisdom is loosely defined as an accurate understanding of how things are and how they function, it would be hard to find disagreement that our economics, both in theory and practice, should be based on that. This is true no matter how profoundly dissimilar or contradictory particular views may be. The disagreements, of course, are about what wisdom actually is.

If we agree that basing economics on wisdom is not in dispute, we might now consider the Mahayana Buddhist view. In that view, wisdom actually *is* compassion or, to put it more precisely, wisdom is inseparable from compassion. But what does this really mean?

Let's not accept such a proposition too easily. It has always been emphasized in the Buddhist tradition that we should not accept ideas without proper analysis. That is especially important in this case, because if it is true, it is so significant. Without proper reflection, we may not really understand what is meant by the two ideas, or in what sense wisdom and compassion can be considered inseparable.

CIVIL ENDOWMENT

In the Standard English dictionary definition, compassion means wishing that others will be free from suffering. This is a perfectly good starting point for discussion. A typical dictionary definition of wisdom is "the ability to discern or judge what is true, right, or lasting; insight." How is it, then, that compassion is an expression of wisdom? Albert Einstein put it this way:

> "A human being is part of a whole, called by us the 'Universe,' a part limited in time and space. He experiences himself, his thoughts and feelings, as something separated from the rest— a kind of optical delusion of his consciousness. This delusion is a kind of prison for us, restricting us to our personal desires and to affection for a few persons nearest us. Our task must be to free ourselves from this prison by widening our circles of compassion to embrace all living creatures and the whole of nature in its beauty."

Einstein clearly points out how our egocentric preoccupation, based on the assumed separation of the subjective self from all that is other, creates a radically limited view of reality. And he brilliantly posits the way out of this self-absorption, which is to empathize with and indeed endorse the points of view and interests of others. With compassion, we not only widen our perspective, we also undermine the duality that is at the root of our delusion. In doing so, compassion becomes a path, a practical method for revealing wisdom.

What this points out is that compassion and wisdom are related in an ongoing causal process. Wisdom causes compassion, and compassion causes wisdom. How is this so? The Buddhist view is that we all possess inherent wisdom, a potential for the fully awakened mind, and that this inherent wisdom is actually the seed of compassion. In that sense, compassion comes from our naturally present wisdom. Then, as compassion is practiced and becomes mature, wisdom is progressively unveiled, and eventually, perfected. This is why it is accurate to say that wisdom and compassion are inseparable, even though the two terms have different meanings.

One of the interesting implications of viewing compassion as a grounding principle in economics, and seeing it as a genuine route to economic wisdom, is that it carries the possibility of bridging the longstanding gap between theory and practice. Although economists of the many ideological camps have built impressive bodies of theory, those theories are generally—and tragically—deficient in practice. The notion that compassion is a practical application of wisdom is reflected in the Mahayana concept of skillful means (*upaya* in Sanskrit). Wisdom is seen as a deep insight into the nature of reality, an insight that is infused with compassion.

But how do we apply that compassion toward helping others? The answer is that we apply it by implementing what are called the Six Perfections: generosity, ethics, tolerance, diligence, meditation/concentration, and wisdom. In our discussion to follow, we will use these six principles as the basis for a set of economic virtues, which together form a very elegant framework for an economics of compassion.

An Expanded Definition of Compassion

Before discussing the implementation of compassion, it would be helpful to go into a bit more detail about what we mean by compassion altogether. This is especially true since it can be argued that there is at least some measure of compassion inherent in all the major systems of economics. The original ideas behind socialism and the free-enterprise system both contained elements of social compassion, though from different angles. The older idea of the "benevolent despot" is another form of compassion in economics, and the more recent concept of the welfare state derives from such an outlook. Even Keynesian macroeconomics, which boils down to rather technocratic government actions around fiscal and monetary policies, carries this intention, since in theory it tries to make the economy better for everyone. Despite the manifest failures of these systems, try thinking about the compassionate intentions behind them—especially the systems with which you strongly disagree.

The definition of compassion we will use for this body of work is more complex than the simple idea of wishing that others do not suffer. It is an expansion or elaboration of that idea. This is needed in part because the idea of economic suffering is in itself complex, and requires careful consideration. At an obvious level, we can say that poverty, lack of opportunity, exploitation, and so on, all constitute economic suffering. Less obvious, however, is the suffering that comes about from having too much and, at the psychological level, from our obsession with obtaining livelihood. As well, what about the suffering we cause others by obtaining our livelihood? And what about the unimaginable suffering that will come to future generations if we destroy the ecosystem of the very planet on which we live? In simplest terms, we can say that economic suffering for a particular person is to be deprived of the things we really need for human life: air, water, food, shelter, clothing, and more complex needs such as medical care, education, and so on.

As we go deeper into thinking about even a very basic sense of economic needs, it becomes clear that, although these needs can be described in terms of the individual, they can really only be obtained in a healthy and well-functioning human society. This is abundantly obvious in the case of the economic implications of war and peace, or of ecological catastrophe versus ecological wellbeing. The very complexity of these questions makes a more detailed working definition of compassion useful.

The description we will use for this book is a summation of what is known in Mahayana Buddhism as *The Four Immeasurables*, which are expressed in terms of aspirations. The first of these is that all beings have happiness and the causes of happiness; the second is that they may have freedom from suffering and causes of suffering; the third is that beings have the higher forms of joy associated with the spiritual path; and the fourth is that they may have the profound equanimity associated with wisdom. This formulation adds considerable depth to the simpler notion of compassion as mere wish for freedom from suffering. The four aspects of the aspiration are called immeasurable because they apply to all beings, and because they are immeasurable in depth and profundity even if we were to have them for just one being—let alone all beings. Thus, we could say that the virtue of truly holding this attitude is "immeasurable to the immeasurable power."

This more elaborate definition of compassion will form the background of our considerations here, because it supports the full range of human aspirations and wisdom. It works well with an economic vision that encompasses a complete and vibrant view of human culture, one that goes beyond mere material sufficiency to areas such as learning, the arts, creativity, and spirituality. Compassion in this expanded sense means helping create the conditions for the flowering, in the highest sense of the word, of individual human beings and of human society as a whole.

An important part of giving rise to compassion is to do so in an unbiased way, which means having an impartial outlook. Often, of course, we human beings display great kindness in our economic behavior toward our close relations, especially family members or members of our own ethnic group, social class, or country. But often the reverse is true for people we regard as "other." We often treat such people with indifference at best, or quite often with varying degrees of exploitation and downright cruelty. To reverse that tendency and refrain from excluding the "other" is an expression of real compassion.

The ability to be fully inclusive, to think in terms of humanity as a whole, as well as to regard each individual impartially, is part of the wisdom potential we all possess. Although we do not all hold this attitude, it is entirely possible for any one of us to do so. The truth is that compassion is inherent to the human mind. It is not specifically a spiritual or religious attitude. It cannot be imposed by law or even custom—although social influence is certainly important.

When we think about an unbiased attitude of compassion, it is interesting to ask if this means caring for "humanity as a whole" or somehow caring for each individual. Really, it needs to be both. Caring for humanity as a whole does mean caring for each individual. But the wholeness or oneness of humanity can also be considered as an object of compassion, abstract as this idea may be—and this point has definite significance in the reasoning to come regarding civil endowment. We need to see that the natural world, human society, and the world economy make up one big interrelated system. We need to do things that heal that system. Compassion is the most essential reason for doing so, and compassion for the whole comes back around to having compassion for each individual.

We also could consider that each of us actually comprises part of humanity's whole. In fact, as we explore things further, we will increasingly see that our individual fate, and hence our individual interests, are utterly tied up with this whole. We can say with real certainty at this point in history that a very significant part of each of our individual economic interests coincides with the interest of the human whole. Conversely, the condition of the human whole affects every individual.

With all that said, generating unbiased compassion may still be a bit of a stretch. Why should we have compassion for terrorists, criminals, or those we think are bad people? In economic terms, I think the best approach to this potential objection is that real evil doers are a definite minority, and we should start by thinking about the vast majority of more ordinary people and try to create good outcomes for them, with the understanding that by creating a healthy, fair economy, we will be helping remove the causes of crime, conflict, and so on.

Taking a spiritual perspective on the same question would depend on one's outlook. The Buddhist point of view would be that we should have compassion for evildoers (along with, of course, those they harm) since those who do evil will suffer greatly for their actions in the future. As well, there is no reason that taking a spiritual attitude of compassion means we in any way accept evil or remain passive toward it. Rejecting a stance of unbiased compassion, simply based on specific cases of wrongdoing, would reflect an inaccurate view of what compassion actually is. Compassion does not mean being weak or ignoring problematic behavior. Practically speaking, it makes sense that if we diffuse the conditions that foster human evil—many of which are economic—we will be curtailing evil to some degree before it happens.

This matter of unbiased compassion is something to be contemplated rigorously. If we do think it over carefully, and it passes muster, so to speak, we will have a stable basis for putting it into practice. Putting compassion into practice does not depend on everyone having compassion, nor does it mean imposing such behavior on anyone. That is not necessary, and indeed it is not possible. On the other hand, if we give it only passing consideration, or some kind of mental "lip service," our attitude will not stand the test of time as we try to put it into action.

The Six Virtues

The view of Mahayana Buddhism is that we begin our journey toward full enlightenment with an aspiration to do so, one that is infused with an attitude of compassion so vast and inclusive that it includes aspiring to help all other beings reach enlightenment. This extraordinary attitude of mind is called aspiration bodhicitta. The actual path of putting that aspiration into practice is called implementation bodhicitta, which consists of the Six Perfections, or *paramitas* in Sanskrit. Paramita can also be translated as "transcendent action," but as an eminent Tibetan master, the late Traleg Rinpoche (1955–2012) points out, this is not meant in an otherworldly sort of way:

> When we say that *paramita* means "transcendent action," we mean it in the sense that actions or attitude are performed in a non-egocentric manner. "Transcendental" does not refer to some external reality, but rather to the way in which we conduct our lives and perceive the world—either in an egocentric or a non-egocentric way. The six *paramitas* are concerned with the effort to step out of the egocentric mentality.[2]

---

2) Ray, Reginald A. (ed.) (2004). *In the Presence of Masters: Wisdom from 30 Contemporary Tibetan Buddhist Teachers*. Boston, Massachusetts, USA: Shambhala.

Therefore, we can say that the Six Perfections are actions that go beyond egocentricity. Once we have developed an unbiased compassion for all beings, and the resolve to work for universal enlightenment, the perfections are presented as the means to walk that path and accomplish that goal.

These Six Perfections can be very directly applied to positive economic behavior to create an elegant description of an economics of compassion, expressed in terms of the following six virtues: generosity, ethics, non-aggression, diligence, focusing, and wisdom. These six virtues are named almost identically to the translations of the names of the paramitas from Sanskrit or Tibetan. The only real exception is the fifth perfection, meditation, which has been modified to "focusing" in its presentation as an economic virtue.

Generosity

The fact that generosity is a fundamental virtue is easy to understand, and it certainly pertains directly to economics. It is a good starting point for the recognition that these six virtues are absolutely intrinsic to economic civilization. Without the generosity of parents to children in particular, and people to their close relations in general, human society as we know it would simply not exist. Although such generosity does carry with it the attachment and obligation that go with such relationships, the fact is that it is most typically also an expression of love and commitment. The fact that generosity of this sort is so pervasive, so ubiquitous, and so natural demands that we acknowledge it in our economic thinking.

The problem is that, with a few exceptions, modern economists have generally not found a comfortable way to incorporate generosity into their theories at all. Although modern economic theory is generally flummoxed by generosity, or takes pains to ignore it completely, that is not the case for early Western thinkers. The Western scholastic tradition that comes down to us from Aristotle, St. Augustine, and Thomas Aquinas clearly pointed out that economic exchanges can be grouped in three categories: gift, theft, and reciprocal exchange. Among modern economists, Kenneth Boulding stands out with his development of a whole branch of the discipline called grants economics. Classical and neoclassical thinkers have focused almost exclusively on the exchange economy, emphasized self-interest as an organizing (and indeed an optimizing) principle. Modern leftist commentators have historically tended to see economic inclusion as a political right, not as something that is particularly to be achieved by generosity. There is also the whole messy question of non-monetized transactions. Hazel Henderson has famously described the "love economy," as practiced most notably by women throughout history, and the importance thereof. The fact that such a vast amount of economic benefit is simply given away by unpaid or underpaid workers makes it very hard for most economists to work with. They like nice neat things that have numbers attached to them so they can put them into equations.

If we start with individual economic behavior, it is clear that generosity is a clear and valid way to practice the economics of compassion. As we expand our consideration outward to economic behavior in society, we arrive at the practice of charity and philanthropy. These types of activities play a huge role in human society—and increasingly so. People give so much, in so many ways, to people they don't know at all, and often for little or no recognition, that it is simply amazing. Although there are many shortcomings to charity and philanthropy, including the general criticism that it merely tends to perpetuate the existing system of "haves and have nots," we still need to recognize that this type of economics of compassion has existed for a very long time.

Whether human generosity can be further mobilized to decisively address critical global problems is one of the great questions of our time. The question is not just whether it can be mobilized, or how to mobilize it, but most pointedly, how the natural generosity of humanity can *be utilized* to transform the economic landscape. As we will see, this is one of the vital points of discussion in Civil Endowment theory.

A contemporary expression of generosity that should be noted is the phenomena of crowdfunding. Kickstarter, the largest platform for such campaigns, has reportedly raised over one billion dollars for 135,000 different creative projects since it was founded in 2009. Although donors may receive certain rewards or recognition for their help, crowdfunding is essentially a gift-economy process. The success of Kickstarter and many similar platforms points to the power of personal networks, the social dimension of the Internet—and most fundamentally to our natural inclination to want to help one another without any clear-cut reciprocal return.

Another dimension of material generosity is one not normally associated with generosity at all, namely, conservation. If you think about it, what is the implication of not wasting resources? First of all, *you* save money. But beyond that, that resource is available for someone else. Thus we can view conservation as an expression of generosity. Conservation, in its environmental dimensions, also relates to another major category mentioned in traditional Buddhist accounts of generosity, namely, the "generosity of protection." Clearly, if you protect someone from harm in some way, you have given them a great gift—perhaps the gift of life itself. The relevance of this to our contemporary economic activity is this: environmentally positive behavior is a form of generosity. Although this may seem to be just another way of talking about it, it is of significance. Any environmentalist knows of the great challenge of shifting human behavior (whether individual or organizational) toward more positive environmental actions. Often there is a lot of guilt and blame attached to the old wasteful and destructive ways of doing things, and a lot of authoritarian righteousness associated with it all. At the same time, the real level of compliance and the willingness to change is rather shallow. We need new ways of encouraging each other to behave more in harmony with the planet and with a future that isn't going to be a total catastrophe. Framing the protection of humanity from environmental harm as a form of generosity is a positive way of approaching this, and it brings out the natural human heroism that we all possess.

The third traditional category of generosity can be called the "generosity of truth." It is actually generous to study, to contemplate, to look for answers, and to communicate those answers. It is generous to courageously proclaim the sorts of "inconvenient truths" we all need to hear. Again, seeing this as generosity may just be a different way of framing actions that like-minded people already accept and honor. But again, if we see it in a new way, we may find new strength to practice this form of generosity. Often there is a strong flavor of criticism and anger in our proclamation of truth. There is certainly blame enough to go around, but seeing the communication of truth as a form of generosity makes it more likely that we will temper it with understanding and kindness. Perhaps the truth we share will have more of a chance to be heard and acted upon.

Ethical Discipline

Ethics and morality are deeply intertwined with economic behavior throughout history. If you study the subject of economic history, you will see fascinating shifts in what has been considered ethical or moral. For example, in the Europe's Middle Ages, making a profit "for its own sake" was deemed immoral—and in fact illegal—by the Catholic Church. Lending money at interest (usury) was also banned, and some cultures have continued such a prohibition to this day. There are also certain basic principles that can be regarded as universal across cultures and history, such as the injunction against stealing.

In any case, what this discussion may contribute to this vast body of thought and convention may just be a few significant points of emphasis. The first is simply a consideration of *why* we might want to practice ethical conduct. To practice ethical conduct out of compassion is a refreshing shift of emphasis from the heavy shroud of legalistic moralism surrounding the subject. Typically there is an emphasis on morality/immorality in terms of its consequences— which could be legal or spiritual, based on one's point of view.

The Eastern traditions emphasize the inevitable law of karma, which follows us independent of human retribution or even divine judgment. To avoid negative actions out of concern for their impact on one's own future is entirely justified. But even more powerful and profound is to do so out of compassion for others. In some sense, it is also more natural. If you have compassion, you don't steal because you don't want to deprive someone of something that is theirs, not because you may get caught and punished, or suffer from bad karma in future lives. It is direct and simple. Although ethics can be quite complicated, compassion will usually steer us in the right direction.

Buddhism talks about ethics in terms of avoiding negative actions and adopting positive ones, and in intentional actions to benefit others. In economic terms, it is clear that some things to avoid would be stealing, deception, fraud, manipulation, cruelty, and exploitation. On the positive side, we can enact ethical discipline by practicing fairness, honesty, and kindness in economic dealings. Ethics in our personal practice of economic behavior is a very important subject, because we have a high degree of direct control over our own behavior. It is, therefore, an area of personal responsibility.

When we expand our consideration to the broader picture of society generally, we arrive at the essential question of economic justice. It is worth reminding ourselves that considerations of economic justice arise from our views about ethics, and that ethics in the most genuine sense of the word arises from compassion. Therefore I will include a brief discussion of economic justice within this section on ethics.

Economic Justice

Basing justice on ethics leads to a very direct perspective on the subject. And if that ethical attitude is unbiased, it leads directly to a very important principle, that of inclusion. This is a key point for economic justice at our present juncture in history. How do we create fairness for everyone, without destroying fundamental individual rights? The inclusion principle applies not just to people in the present; it is now recognized that it must span the past, present, and future. It is not enough to say, for example, "Well, everyone has a right to own property." (I'm well aware that not all societies provide even this basic right.) That ignores past and present power arrangements. It is fine to talk about the ethics of transactions and dealings in the past and present, laws and regulations, and so on. But if there is no justice for people in the future, how can we say there is justice?

Another important point is that economic justice must respect the whole-system quality of human society and the natural world. This is different from older views about individual versus collective rights. These older systems of thought failed to see the radical interdependence of human society with the natural world. All the real leaders in economic thinking today are keenly aware of the fact that economic justice and environmental justice are inseparable. Taking a whole-system approach in that sense is radically different from collectivist thinking. It does not deny individual rights, but instead extends them to everyone.

Another dimension of ethics could be called the "ethics of post-materialism." To paraphrase a famous quote, we can't cure economic injustice "with the same mentality that created it." Therefore, a fundamental critique of materialism and a realignment of values related to that is an essential part of our ethical engagement. The possibility of relaxing our obsessive drive for material consumption and convenience is a prerequisite for changing our economic way of life and gradually putting human values and human wellbeing first.

It should be clear that there are many aspects of ethics as they pertain to economics that need to be brought up to date. The planetary-level challenges we face, and which are now widely recognized, demand new kinds of thinking. Ethics can be traced back not only to kindness and compassion, but to a respect for the very principle of cause and effect. This must include the consideration of causality operating in whole systems—up to and including the meta-system of the whole of human society in the global ecosystem. To contemplate and engage ourselves in taking compassionate action in relation to this whole system is a very high level of ethical engagement.

Finally, we should not assume that economic justice can or should be achieved by political means alone. In reality, justice is "pre-institutional" in the sense that it encompasses all four domains of human society—i.e., those of government, business, civil society, and the individual. We can each bring about justice on a granular scale by practicing positive ethics in our lives and dealings. We can build those principles into organizations we create and in which we participate.

Non-Aggression

The third of the Six Perfections is *kshanti* in Sanskrit, which is translated as patience, forbearance, or tolerance. The basic point of kshanti as a spiritual quality is not to give rise to anger, even in situations that normally would stimulate anger. Breaking what is often called the "cycle of anger" brings tremendous benefit to oneself and others. The economic virtue that is derived from this perfection could simply be called tolerance, but also, importantly, it could be understood as non-aggression. It is not necessary to go to any length in discussing the tremendous dangers and suffering that anger and hatred bring to humanity. Events on the world stage give us plenty of examples of that every day.

In economics, the play of anger may be a bit more subtle, but it is also extraordinarily corrosive in effect. Closely related to anger are jealousy and competitiveness. In this context, we are referring to competitiveness in the negative psychological sense of the word. Competition is commonly touted as a positive phenomenon in economics, but the reality is that even if healthy economic competition has some benefits, it is still typically admixed with unhealthy psychological qualities. The topic of competition at a basic level deserves a much more in-depth discussion than we can have here, but suffice to say that cooperation is better.

The virtue of tolerance and non-aggression in economic life can be incredibly healing and transformative. It makes cooperation possible. Cooperation and fair competition are hard to achieve because we as human beings carry a great deal of negativity towards those we perceive as other. On the other hand, there is a growing realization among at least some of us that there ultimately is no "other;" we're all in this together. Despite this growing awareness, non-aggression is a tough one. Those of us who seek economic justice often develop a great deal of anger toward those who work against it. And we think, "If we don't get angry, how are we going to motivate ourselves and others to change things?" These are hard questions, and they don't deserve simplistic answers. However, it is possible to envision and create economic systems that do not support aggression and harmful competition, and do emphasize cooperation.

Generally speaking, it is rather radical to mention the notion of non-aggression in an economic context in today's world. It seems like a foreign concept. It may bring up the thought that if "we" behave with non-aggression, then "they" will take advantage of us. Generally speaking, this topic of economic non-aggression is worthy of a tremendous amount of thought and discussion. If appropriate ways of enacting non-aggression can be implemented, it could bring us to a key turning point in economic history.

Diligence

When we talk about diligence or exertion as an economic virtue, it does not simply mean working hard. It means applying hard work and perseverance in the context of truly positive and skillful ways of working, ways that benefit others and avoid harm. In fact, it can take a lot of work just to find modes of livelihood that are not harmful. A great deal of research is going on these days—for example, into how to design all manner of industrial processes in ways that cause less harm to the environment. That is a good example of proper exertion.

Improper diligence, of course, happens all the time. People work tremendously hard to strip the world of its resources, to exploit the work of others, and to steal. In the movie *Heat*, Robert DeNiro plays a master criminal who works with tremendous skill, meticulous planning, and great personal discipline. That's a fine example of the opposite of what is meant here by diligence.

Diligence means "taking joy in virtue."

Unfortunately, all such examples are not fictional. It is interesting that so often the people who have good intentions for the world, and possess gentleness, and ethics, often don't work as hard as the crooks. For better or worse, quite literally, it takes diligence to get something done.

The traditional Buddhist definition of diligence in this context is "taking joy in virtue." I have always found this to be a challenging description, because I have tended to see work as something you have to do—but maybe you don't feel like it. I think the point here is the genuineness of our engagement.

If you really want to see something positive done, you will take strong satisfaction in doing it. Certainly, there is satisfaction in bringing a job to completion, so if we bring that feeling into the moment of the work, we can see how "taking joy in virtue" applies. However, this whole point really brings into focus the need for meaningful work. If we are doing work that is harmful or unsatisfying, it is certainly hard to take joy in it. Therefore, one of the implications of diligence as an economic virtue is the value of creating and promoting work that *does* bring joy and satisfaction.

Focus

Among the Mahayana paramitas, the fifth is called *dhyana* in Sanskrit. This term literally means meditation or concentration in English. It involves the practice of training one's mind at a basic level. It means focusing the mind in the sense of concentration, but also taming the mind to reduce the influence of harmful psychological patterns. The stability and clarity of mind that arise from meditation are necessary conditions for the insights that characterize the sixth paramita, which is called *prajna* (wisdom or discernment). How might this be applied to economics?

When interpreted as an economic virtue, focusing carries many of the same implications that the focusing aspect of basic meditation practice does within the Buddhist path. Focusing here means developing and having the mental presence and direction that enables us to do anything properly. It is the natural focus of work, study and learning, planning and reflection, and all the work of the mind that pertains to economic thought. Without focus, the human mind is ruled by confusion and will fail to see things clearly or get anything useful done. Therefore, focusing can be understood as a process of disciplining the mind to promote stability and precise attention as a basis for economic integrity in work, consumer behavior, and business behavior.

Without focus, the human mind is ruled by confusion.

Integrity of work is perhaps the simplest part of this to understand: mental focus is an ongoing requirement in order to get anything done. Since we are framing all this in the context of compassion, we might ask how "doing the job right" would be an act of compassion. It becomes clear if we think about the people who drive buses and trains or fly planes, or when we consider medical people, teachers, and financial professionals. In fact, all types of work affect others. How well we do a job can, in many cases, be a matter of life and death. Proper focus and attention are required to do the job right.

In consumer behavior, it is interesting to note that having a focused and trained mind will help us avoid being swayed and influenced by advertising and marketing messages of all kinds, including peer pressure. It presents the possibility of being centered in economic behavior. The old-fashioned term for this is being "sensible." Being sensible in today's world doesn't always mean buying the cheaper product. It may mean not buying something at all, or buying a more expensive product that's better for the environment, or comes from a more socially responsible manufacturer. Having the judgment and character to make such decisions requires a stable mind. A stable mind comes from focusing.

In business behavior, the main point to be noted is that focus brings about the penetration necessary to make correct decisions. By correct decisions, I mean responsible decisions. And in the context of the economics of compassion, a responsible decision is one that is responsible to all humanity. That's a tall order, of course, but without the appropriate mental focus, we wouldn't have a chance to make such decisions. We wouldn't even have the ability to make correct decisions, say, for the sake of our own business in the short term.

An even broader application of focus is in the general process of mind training needed for stabilizing compassion altogether. The term mind training is used quite specifically here. One of the very significant sets of practical instruction that comes to us through the Tibetan tradition is a system called *lojong*, which literally means "mind training." Its emphasis is on making the attitude of compassion for all beings one of stable focus and commitment. This system is a vital part of all the major lineages of Tibetan Buddhism, and it has been championed by the great contemporary teachers of that tradition, such as His Holiness the Dalai Lama, Pema Chodron, and many others.

The strong emphasis given to turning compassion into a genuine discipline highlights the importance of really establishing such an attitude in an unshakable way. Usually, our compassion is limited in several ways. As mentioned above, we generally have compassion for people we like. According to Buddhist teachers, this may not be compassion at all—or if it is, it is compassion mixed with attachment. The defect in that case, of course, is that we are biased, and our minds very easily switch over to cruelty towards those we dislike. The other problem is that our compassion is sporadic. Sometimes we think very kind thoughts and try to do nice things, but just as often we behave with more or less total self-absorption.

Having a stable outlook of compassion does not mean living a life of martyrdom or ascetic sainthood, but it does mean finding some consistency in attitude and behavior. It means remembering compassion when things get complicated. It involves extending compassion to people we really don't like. And most essentially, it means applying compassion on a universal basis, in an unbiased way. All this becomes possible only by making compassion an object of focus, and by carefully training ourselves. By doing so, compassion eventually becomes thoroughly familiar. It becomes part of our very character.

Finally, we can understand mental focus as being a condition for generating insight and wisdom concerning economics. The fact is that economics is a complex subject and presents a vast array of conceptual information—much of which is confusing and contradictory. This is certainly true for the main schools of economics that have come down to us in the European tradition. They are seriously at odds, and indeed they have been the source of deep conflict in society.

We may be in an era of history in which the "free market" system seems to have won the conflict with socialism/communism, but that appearance masks a deeper fragmentation of actual theory and practice. And the evident defects and potentially catastrophic flaws of a market system are glaringly obvious at this point in history, despite the ascendancy of the system itself. In practice, the complexities of a globalized economy in crisis require a clarity that does not come from mere information or from following the opinions of so-called experts. Those who will provide real leadership in economics are not only going to be the academics (learned as they are) or the think-tank pundits of C-Span (who often have strong ideological biases), or the hired-hand economists of investment banks and brokerage firms (who invariably have deep conflicts of interest). Much has been said of the failures of economics as a profession, and much of it is deserved. Although it is in many ways unfair to blame economists for the state of the world economy today, is still reasonable to expect that those who study and profess knowledge of the subject evolve in their insight and their capacity to help humanity.

Therefore, and however we come to the study of economics, bringing a strong, focused, and compassionate mind to its contemplation will make it possible for our study to be of positive service to humanity. Through such a focus, we can come to develop economic wisdom.

Wisdom

One point that is always emphasized in Buddhist teachings on the Six Perfections is that for each of the first five Perfections to really be transcendent, they each need to be infused with wisdom. This is quite easy to understand if we think about the pitfalls that can occur if we practice the virtues in unskillful ways. An extreme example of generosity without wisdom would be giving a gun to someone who is suicidal. There are plenty of less obvious ways that generosity can be practiced unwisely, many of them quite subtle. The same is true for misguided ethics, tolerance, and so on. It is hard to generalize about this because one of the key aspects of wisdom is that it is situational.

Chogyam Trungpa Rinpoche gave a wonderful definition of wisdom. He said that it was "intelligence plus presence." Being intelligent isn't enough. You have to be there. It is like the difference between knowing that you shouldn't walk in front of an oncoming car, and actually paying attention when crossing the street. At that level, it is pretty clear that we all have basic wisdom, at least most of the time. We wouldn't live through the day if we didn't. Because this basic wisdom is so situational, I will not say more about it here, except that it is a matter of personal responsibility to always try to put it into play. We must not live and act blindly, no matter how good our intentions.

Wisdom is "intelligence plus presence."

Then we could ask, "Well, what is wisdom as it applies specifically to economics?" This will be the subject of our next chapter, where we will look at economic wisdom in two major categories: post-materialism, and co-centricity. But before we move on, let's return to a question posed at the very beginning of this chapter, namely, "If we do practice an economics of compassion with these six virtues, are there good economical outcomes?" In short, is it economical?

For those who value compassion, it may seem unnecessary to ask whether its outcomes are "economical." Granted, if we see compassion as an end in itself, it would be crass to argue, for example, that it also makes us richer. But the question of economic outcomes is much more complex than that. There are two fundamental reasons to make an argument for certain efficiencies arising from the six virtues. The first reason is to influence our very notion of what is economical. In particular, materialist and atomistic ways of thinking have so shaped economic thought for many centuries that we have a very hard time looking at things in other ways.

The second reason is even more fundamental. When carefully examined, the qualities and outcomes of economic compassion expressed in these six virtues will be understood to be absolutely fundamental to civilization. We tend to take them for granted, but we lament when they are absent. Therefore, the ultimate reason for discussing the economic outcomes of the six virtues is to explicitly point out—and to celebrate for that matter—how these six virtues are at the very roots of civilized behavior in an economic sense.

We have spoken of how generosity in families underlies society, but it is also obvious that ethics and non-aggression make any sort of trade or organized enterprise possible. Without some basic level of trust and tolerance for each other, we would be nothing better than snarling beasts in the wild.

Cynics, perhaps, will point to the delicate play of self-interest that creates a veneer of civilization, or to the fact that laws and regulations are needed to keep things in balance. That being as it may, it is still true that the norms we establish and expect are in keeping with the basic virtues, especially ethics. They are norms because they are absolutely necessary, and that remains true whether we practice them because of custom and law, or out of our own wisdom. As we go deeper into the wisdom aspect of economics, we will see the need and the possibility of going beyond a legalistic or political mentality in addressing the problems of our times, and of establishing a true economics of compassion on the basis of civil society. If these virtues are really what make us truly human, why not take that principle to its logical completion? This, in essence, is what has motivated the development of civil endowment theory.

CHAPTER FOUR

The Principles of Economic Wisdom

L ET'S START BY THINKING ABOUT ECONOMIC WISDOM IN very simple terms. What qualities should we expect of it? If we are to find a *correct* way of seeing things, we can say that, first, we must understand how to go beyond an *incorrect* way of seeing things. Second, we need to have a positive sense of the actual characteristics of the correct way of seeing things. Though very simple, this is a start—something to build upon.

We also need to think about how we arrive at wisdom. From the Buddhist point of view, we all possess some degree of intrinsic wisdom, along with the potential for its full flowering. Wisdom at its most basic level is inherent in the basic awareness that we all possess. If that is true, what we need to do is bring that seed of wisdom to maturity. We can do that by clearing away our confusion, and cultivating our awareness of how things really are.

If we take a cue from the traditional Mahayana Buddhist perspective on developing wisdom, the clear implication would be that we can develop our potential for economic wisdom by establishing the right attitude (one of unbiased compassion), and then by effectively practicing the five economic virtues, which all lead to wisdom. These virtues are both the expression of wisdom, and a means for maturing it further and further.

Each of the five virtues (generosity, ethics, non-aggression, diligence, and focusing) is essential in deepening and enacting wisdom. By actually putting these qualities into practice, we refine and strengthen our initial shift in attitude, and learn by experience. In particular, the fifth virtue, focusing, functions as an inflexion point toward wisdom. The psychological training and intellectual activities necessary to bring wisdom to maturity are all included in the virtue of focusing. These include observation, research, and contemplation of our world, along with study and reflection concerning the teachings and ideas about economics that have been passed down to us. Focusing also includes the mind training necessary to accomplishing all the virtues properly, and it stabilizes and sustains the unbiased attitude of compassion and aspiration we generated at the beginning.

Focusing functions as an inflexion point toward wisdom.

Obviously, much more could be said about the process of cultivating economic wisdom. But here we will move on from this brief overview to the qualities of economic wisdom itself. Of course, wisdom is something more than a view that can be presented conceptually. It is some sort of quality of mind, of understanding, or knowledge. At its heart, wisdom is always a direct experience, but we can also try to describe that experience.

I have come to understand the nature of economic wisdom in two broad categories, which are complementary and non-contradictory, and which fulfill the two requirements mentioned at the beginning of the this chapter: cutting through incorrect views, and expressing a correct view in positive terms. The two categories are: **post-materialism** and **co-centricity**. Post-materialism is the outcome of refuting and abandoning our deluded thinking and ways of acting. Co-centricity is a way of describing the seeing of things as they are, and points toward actions that are truly beneficial.

There are several perspectives from which we could explore these wisdom principles, such as personal attitudes and behaviors, economic theories, and philosophical views. However, the unifying principle, the perspective that touches on all these points of view is the psychological one. How do our minds engage with economics at every level—all the way from the day-to-day journey of livelihood to the more rarified realms of theory, policy, activism, and innovation? We will touch on all aspects of consideration, and keep coming back to the characteristics of our mental engagement in this discussion of economic wisdom.

After exploring post-materialism and co-centricity, we will summarize our subject with a consideration of outcomes, not just of cultivating and practicing wisdom, but of all of the six virtues which, as they mature, can be seen as a unified practice of compassion and wisdom.

Post-Materialism

By its very subject matter, economics deals with what we refer to as "the material world." Specifically, it looks at how we meet our needs for the physical necessities of life, such as food, water, shelter, and clothing. As civilization has become more complex, our engagement with material things and the work associated with them have become increasingly complex. Due to the scientific and technological revolutions of the last few centuries, our human powers in relation to the world around us have increased so greatly that it is not surprising that we are now said to be in an age of materialism. It seems only natural for humanity to become so intensely involved with our newfound abilities. At the same time, materialism itself is somewhat mysterious. It is not necessarily a conscious attitude, and it exists at various levels of subtlety.

At the most basic and personal level, materialism is a basic pattern of attachment. We have a strong psychological involvement with acquiring and possessing certain things—whether we need them or not. As a social phenomenon, materialism is often called consumerism. Economic materialism is responsible for the view, both within the discipline of economics and in society generally, that "more is better." That is the economics you generally see on TV or in the business section of newspapers. Critics have labeled this sort of materialism "affluenza." The implication of that term, of course, is that it is a disease. In simplest terms, if we then somehow get over this disease, that is post-materialism, at least at the personal level. Of course, various individuals and groups at different points in history have gotten this point to varying degrees. All religions, for example, more or less promote the view that we need to get past our materialism. We typically give lip service to socially received messages against materialism, and ascribe to clichés like "money isn't everything." Yet in the realm of economics—and certainly business—most of what drives people is "more is better." The same is usually true for our personal behavior as consumers.

If we take a deeper look at materialism, taking a sympathetic view toward the human condition, it is clear how easy it is to think that way. We are all in some sense natural materialists. It accords with our natural, naïve realism and with the rawness of our needs and wants. One way to easily understand post-materialism is to see that materialism is something that we all instinctively ascribe to, and that we have to grow out of it. When we do that, we are post-materialists; we have developed some wisdom. It would be a bit fishy to say, "I'm a non-materialist." It is better to admit that we've been there with materialism, both individually and socially. To whatever degree we are able to put our materialism behind us, we will be able to focus on basic human values and quality of life.

If we examine materialism closely, we can arrive at the insight that at its core there is a psychological pattern of solidification of experience, both internal and external. In fact, the internal and external aspects of that solidification are part of the same pattern. This is the classic conclusion of Buddhist and other non-dual psychologies. From the point of view of an assumed solid self or ego, we create a psychological point of view that solidifies what is assumed to be external to that perspective. The attachment and fixation that creates and sustains that assumed duality is the very stuff of our confusion. Subject and object are in reality interdependent, but we substantialize the two poles, simply on the basis of each other. In short, the solidity of ourselves and the "external" world is a mental construction. To describe this general pattern, I use the term psychological materialism.[1]

Psychological materialism refers to the mind's solidification of both external and internal things, and our entrenchment within that solidity. Thus, it refers to our sense of the materiality of natural phenomena, but also to the solidity that we attach to internal experiences, states of mind, emotions, and concepts.

The key insight here is that the solidification of seemingly external objects of mind into "things" that are supposedly real and

---

1) The term "psychological materialism" was used by Chogyam Trungpa Rinpoche, who was one of the pioneers in bringing Buddhism to the Western world. Trungpa Rinpoche was more famous, of course, for the term "spiritual materialism." I use the term psychological materialism in a specific way that is idiosyncratic to my own body of thought, and I don't attempt or claim to use it exactly the same way that Trungpa Rinpoche did. However, the way we will use the term here is definitely derived from Buddhist psychology in general.

truly existent is performed by the mind itself. Now, there are a lot of pitfalls that can come about if we understand this superficially, but certainly it is good as a start to at least question our assumptions about the world of our experiences. If we do not question the assumptions we make, we fall into the realm of naive realism, which means we are firmly in the grip of psychological materialism. In fact, we've been there a very long time, according to Buddhism. We could go one step further here and say that psychological materialism is one way of characterizing what the Buddhists call samsara, because samsara is a mind-created solidification of what is not inherently solid in reality.

The implications of the psychological nature of materialism are quite interesting. For one thing, if materialism is simply a mental attitude, and a confused one at that, why can't we just drop it right here and now? Well, if we were truly decisive, we *could* drop it as a conceptual view, if we had really repudiated it internally. But unfortunately the mind is not as simple as that. Even if the abandonment of materialism is a good idea, we still have to contend with all the habits of mind, and instincts at play—the fundamental entrenchment of samsara. If psychological materialism is synonymous with samsara, then from a Buddhist point of view, fully transcending it is no easy endeavor.

However, developing a post-materialist orientation is not as rigorous as all that. If we were to talk about going beyond psychological materialism in general, it would mean simply the intention or commitment to not letting ourselves be ruled by the negative patterns of mind that keep us in a state of ignorance and suffering. In more economic terms, it would mean not letting materialism of the economic sort rule our minds and behaviors. At the policy level, it would mean not letting wealth and simple greed

CIVIL ENDOWMENT

for "more, more, more," rule the day. At the theoretical level of economics, it would involve not getting caught up in the "materialism of symbolic representation," which refers to dwelling on abstract representations of economic matters to the detriment of addressing what really matters in human terms. The main way that this symbolic materialism operates is through the dominance of quantitative analysis over qualitative or normative assessments. This is why you constantly hear about the need for "metrics" in any kind of policy discussion. There is actually no problem with metrics or quantitative discussions, as long as they are framed in a valid qualitative context. At that point, metrics become useful tools. Otherwise they are destructive distractions.

I would like to take the discussion of post-materialism to one more level, which is related to this "materialism of symbolic representation." Perhaps it is not too hard to see the limitations of viewing economics through an entirely mathematical lens. Though this has been a trend—and is something of a victorious trend nowadays—there has always been resistance to it, and there have been many countervailing voices. But the other aspect of psychological materialism that we need to recognize is that of conceptuality itself. The formation of concepts by our minds represents a subtle solidification or "materialization," which, if unrecognized, is ultimately very problematic.

Therefore, an important aspect of post-materialist analysis is to question and progressively cut through our conceptual entrenchment altogether. At the very least, we could come to see that, "a concept is just a concept." Generally, we leave our conceptual views unquestioned—at least those views that we believe to be correct. The approach of post-materialism is not to reject the fact that conceptual thinking is valuable, nor does it try to specify or define whatever may be "beyond words." As a first step, it just recognizes concepts as concepts. And from that, it recognizes the limitations of conceptuality in two areas, namely that we can easily be mistaken in our views and, more fundamentally, that our conceptualization in and of itself constitutes a veil over a deeper way of seeing.

When I form a conceptual view that something is, say, good or bad, there is some possibility that I am wrong. What I think is bad might be good, and so on. That is what is meant by the idea that a concept may be mistaken. (Of course, we also need to see that "correct" and "incorrect" are conceptual evaluations as well.)

We question whether ideas are correct or incorrect all the time. We certainly do this with others, and (perhaps more helpfully), we can do it with our own views. But we typically don't question the validity of the conceptuality itself. The idea of "concept as a veil" points to this more fundamental level of limitation. It means that our thinking about things is always some kind of abstraction. Therefore, even if my description or evaluation of something is correct as opposed to incorrect, it is still conceptual. At least potentially, it gets in the way of seeing directly. This is true even though conceptual thinking is also an expression of our intelligence.

Seeing thoughts as "just thoughts" brings freedom and spaciousness.

The post-materialist analysis simply points this all out. It does not try to establish a "correct" conceptual view as opposed to an "incorrect" one. Instead, it acknowledges the limitations of the conceptual view altogether. The result of this is a kind of freedom and a sense of spaciousness.

At that point, it is helpful to really establish such an insight from an experiential point of view, rather than just jumping to whatever implications that might have. The habit of conceptualizing experience is a very strong one. It is very quick and self-justifying. For that reason, it is not enough just to see that conceptualization is a veil. We need to gain some experience of that fact.

That is one reason that we are exploring economic wisdom in two parts, because each of the two aspects represents not only a way of thinking, but also a journey of development. We need to develop our appreciation of post-materialism and co-centricity concurrently.

With post-materialism, it is clearly not enough to say, "Concepts have limitations" and then keep on talking, any more than it is OK to say, "consumerism is bad" and then keep on shopping. It is also not entirely helpful to say, "Certain ideas we have about economics are invalid" and then just replace them with other ideas. The kind of space and freedom that could arise from effectively contemplating post-materialism is one from which creativity and insight might emerge. But there is no guarantee of something good coming of it if we merely contemplate it conceptually. We need to bring it into our direct experience. This process of seeing our psychological materialism, and seeing past it, is an ongoing one. We can't just renounce it, sign some sort of pledge, and move on. And when we get into the co-centric phase of the explanation of economic wisdom, we have to remain circumspect about the conceptual veil, even if the concepts involved are correct or helpful.

It is important to see post-materialism as a cutting through, an abandonment of our psychological materialism. It does not establish some sort of alternative dogma that we can then latch onto with more psychological materialism. We need to respect our minds, not just for their wisdom potential, but also for their tendency to regress, to co-opt ideas, and to re-emerge with a new, more sophisticated brand of materialism.

With that in mind, just what is it that we see that cuts through our psychological materialism? The insight that does the job is that of interdependence at all levels: societal, economic, environmental, and—most essentially—at the phenomenological level of subject and object. This insight, which unifies our subjective mind and the world of experience into a profoundly contextual understanding, marks the transition to the second aspect of economic wisdom, co-centricity.

Co-Centricity

As we have seen, post-materialism is a kind of gateway level of economic wisdom in the sense that it helps untangle our confusion around the way things *appear to be* at various levels. It has a quality of journey to it, in the sense that we will gradually approach its deepest insights through practice and experience. Co-centricity, then, is the aspect of wisdom that is more focused on seeing the way things *actually are.* These two aspects of wisdom are mutually supportive, since clearing away our misconceptions about how things seem to be makes room for seeing how things really are.

Since the term "co-centric" is not a standard one, it would be helpful to begin by discussing the way we will use it here. As far as I know, this is a genuinely new usage in relation to economics. The term is used in geometry and engineering to mean something similar but not identical to "concentric," and it pops up occasionally in articles and blogs (sometimes, it would seem, as an erroneous spelling of concentric). It is not a new term, although I actually dreamed it up myself quite a few years ago. I was looking for a term that means "sharing a mutual center" but in a looser way than my understanding of "concentric."

I have come to use this term in relation to economics in a very broad way, actually, and even have used it as a label for the whole historical trend and body of work in economics, starting most famously with E.F. Schumacher, but probably more properly dating back somewhat earlier to Kenneth Boulding's work in systems theory.

Here we are using it as a description of economic wisdom which, in keeping with its meaning, encompasses a complete description of the subject, since ultimately, post-materialism and co-centricity are themselves, well, co-centric. They contain each other and co-exist harmoniously without losing their specific qualities.

Co-centricity points to a whole array of meanings, from the tangible to the highly abstract. For example, as human beings, we are co-centric with the natural world. Individuals are co-centric within social systems. Social systems themselves display a high degree of co-centricity with other social systems. Think of a family, a town, a region, and a nation. They contain each other, yet have their own defining characteristics.

The symbolic economy of money and price is co-centric with the tangible economy of "stuff." The term brings together meanings such as "interdependent," integral," and "inclusive." It relates to the simultaneous co-abiding of parts and wholes, and of systems and their components. At a more esoteric level, we can speak of the interpenetration or inter-manifestation of phenomena or, to use a term pioneered by Thich Nhat Hahn, interbeing.

When we think about all these terms that have been used, we can get a sense of the co-centricity of meaning. Although all these terms do not each mean exactly the same thing, they share a "center," in the abstract sense of the word. They are co-centric. The center they share is not some other word or concept. Ultimately speaking, co-centric wisdom is the actual wisdom that sees things correctly, and all the terms involved are simply ways that people have tried to express it.

In practical terms, we can summarize the essence of co-centricity with the notion of inclusion. Inclusion encompasses a compassionate social ideal, and it also points to the full range of matters that need to be included in economic analysis and policy. It has long been pointed out by the pioneers of "alternative economics" such as E. F. Schumacher, Hazel Henderson, Herman Daly, and many others that economics as a profession has tended to isolate itself from human values altogether. Hence Schumacher's famous subtitle ". . . *economics as if people mattered.*"

The other well-documented problem with economics in its orthodox form is that it has developed in its own intellectual "silo," which of course is a problem with academic disciplines generally. Every discipline needs to have its area of inquiry and scope of analysis, but this is something that can be taken to extremes, and economics has done so in the extreme. Although it is more difficult to create abstract theories—especially neat, mathematical ones— if you include everything and exclude nothing, the unfortunate fact is that you really *do* need to include everything. The fact that mainstream neoclassical economics has tended to exclude factors like social justice, the environment, or other messy qualitative factors makes it at best a crippled discipline capable only of the most incomplete of answers.

Of course, this is by no means merely a matter of academic concern. We have come to a point in history where economic issues affect the very survival of our species. It is critically important that the discipline of economics rises to the challenge and the urgency of our times. Therefore, economics needs a comprehensive or universal scope of attention: it needs to be co-centric. This is the only way to create a truly successful economics, one that will offer any sort of helpful answers and solutions to the grave human challenges we face. From that point of view, using the term "alternative economics" to describe an economics that is concerned with the environment and human justice is stupid and insulting. In particular, we need a new mainstream that refutes and replaces neoclassical economics with systems of thought that are more suited to economics as a social discipline (as opposed to its pretension to be a science) and which have socially beneficial ramifications.

It should be noted here that co-centric economics is not a term I'm using exclusively for my own ideas, but rather for any economics that fits the characteristics of co-centricity. In practical terms, any economics that is genuinely concerned with social justice, environmental protection, and truly inclusive theory could be considered co-centric. As such, it would include much of the alternative economic theoretical work done in the last 50 years or so. From that point of view, co-centric economics is the body of work into which I would wish my own to fall, without particularly trying to co-opt anyone else's work—or for that matter branding them with my own label.

With that said, let us examine more directly the qualities of co-centric wisdom. For example, what would it look like to see things in terms of radical inclusion? At a social level, this takes us back to unbiased compassion. Such an attitude, by its very definition, includes everyone. The only way to make an honest aspiration based on that attitude would be to wish for everyone to have economic sufficiency and genuine opportunity. In taking such an attitude, there is no need to stipulate some sort of enforced equality of outcomes, which is utterly unrealistic and indeed unfair. But aspirations for universal sufficiency and opportunity are inescapable outcomes of true social inclusion. If that is so, we have a basis for talking about economic justice as well. Economic justice means sufficiency and opportunity—for everybody. It is not a question of whether these things are "realistic." If we take them seriously, it is our job to make them realistic. Going along with that, we would have to also admit that future generations are worthy of our compassion and inclusion as well.

Another characteristic of co-centric wisdom is to think in terms of whole systems. Economic theorists have been thinking in terms of systems for a long time, but they have tended to ignore the idea of *whole* systems. The co-centric imperative, again, is to be fully inclusive. The obvious factor that comes to mind here is the natural world. Up till fairly recently (say the mid-20th century), the natural world (especially as a whole system) was viewed as more or less irrelevant in economic analysis. Thankfully, that is beginning to change. I don't know if we can change our collective economic behavior radically enough, and in time, to save civilization—in particular from the ravages of climate change. But clearly, we have to try.

In that regard, we should recognize that a very important challenge in the quest for wisdom is the topic of causality. For economics to be any sort of really useful discipline, we must recognize both the theoretical and practical principles of the workings of causality, and put them into play to address the deep challenges we face. The synergistic principles of post-materialism and co-centricity bring many resources to bear on this question. It is well beyond the scope of this discussion to lay out a general theory of causality in economic systems, but we will examine causality in some detail in Chapter Six, as we make a case for the usefulness of civil endowments.

One area, however, in which we could contemplate causality here, and in very general terms, is in thinking about the outcomes of practicing the six virtues. Understanding the nature of these outcomes is an expression of seeing clearly. It is wisdom. It is also a great motivation to actually practice the six virtues. The six virtues are general and qualitative in nature, and therefore, we can properly speak about general and qualitative outcomes. We should also preface this discussion with the point that the outcomes of the virtues, if practiced in an authentic way, are really limitless. Therefore, anything we might say about them is just a sliver or glimpse of what could be described. With all that in mind we can say that:

Where there is generosity, there is sufficiency
Where there is ethics, there is justice
Where there is non-aggression, there is cooperation
Where there is diligence, there is productivity
Where there is focus, there is refinement
Where there is wisdom, there is mastery

As noted in the previous chapter, these outcomes could be regarded as efficiencies in a true economic sense of the word—which is not to say in materialist terms. But it is true, isn't it, that these outcomes all speak to wellbeing, abundance, and prosperity? I think this is a wonderful testimony to the fact that they actually *are* virtues. They have good outcomes.

We conclude this section with some thoughts about how we might personally experience and practice the co-centric wisdom. In essence, this means seeing oneself and one's world in a full and accurate context. By "full" I mean we need to see ourselves in terms of where we stand in society, in history, and intellectually and spiritually as well. This is different from what is usually meant by being altruistic or "selfless." The stance we're talking about here is definitely altruistic, and it has generosity and all the other virtues. But it is not self-denying in the sense of passivity. It is not involved with phony mysticism or smug disengagement. We need to see ourselves in our fullness. We are the inheritors of history— for better or worse. We are the ones who can and must uphold society, now and in the future. We are by no means helpless. A great sense of responsibility comes from this outlook. With it, we can also begin to experience some understanding rather than mere anger at the wrongheaded people of our time.

In particular, we need to see our own self-interest as utterly connected with the self-interest of those around us, extending out to the whole world and to the whole of future time. If we are to have any future worth living, we need to work for the future of all. The wisdom I'm trying to describe here comes into being when we see our responsibility—and even more pointedly, our capability. Co-centric wisdom is not some intellectual mumbo jumbo about the oneness of humanity. It is an inescapable, palpable human solidarity. To choose to complete the pursuit of wisdom, to choose compassion, and ultimately to choose responsibility—that is the greatness of the real freedom and capability we humans have. Seeing ourselves in this full context is to be awake—not just to our interbeing with the world, but to the inspiration and commitment that interbeing makes possible.

CHAPTER FIVE

The Leap

Introduction

IN THE PREVIOUS CHAPTER WE EXAMINED A SUBTLE LEVEL OF psychological materialism, that of conceptual fixation, and considered the idea that the loosening of such bonds has a wisdom quality. Freedom from our fixed ideas is indeed a refreshing possibility. Here is an interesting point connected with that: When we read a work of literary fiction, we engage in a "suspension of disbelief," which enables us to enter into the imaginary plot of the story. We willingly immerse ourselves in descriptions of events that we know are not factual. By analogy, when we read non-fiction, it could be said that we need to develop a mirror of that, a "suspension of belief." We could set aside our existing assumptions and formulations, and simply focus on a line of thought on its own terms.

Perhaps this is just an elaborate way of saying that we need to be open minded when considering new ideas, and that this is the only way to give such ideas a fair chance. Just as the wisdom of post-materialism could manifest as an open-mindedness with regard to ideas, we could also apply the co-centric wisdom of an "economics without boundaries," a widening of scope of attention into unfamiliar territory or unusual juxtapositions. Both these attitudes will be helpful in coming to a clear understanding of the civil endowment idea.

This section is an exploration of four key points which, if understood clearly, point to a much greater set of implications than they would have if taken out of mutual context. They are like four steps that, when completed, amount to a leap. Inevitably, these points do, to some degree, also reflect a recapitulation of the process I went through in birthing the idea of civil endowment, although that is not the emphasis here. I have simply tried to organize a presentation of four main "doorways" into the understanding of the civil endowment idea.

As we have seen, the essential conception of civil endowment rests on an analysis and reconsideration of the very idea of capital. But the first point that makes up "the leap" is simply to see how important capital is, and how central a role it plays in a modern economy. When we get that point in focus, we will not only see why the reformation of capital is the key to economic transformation—we will also be motivated to make it happen.

In the second point, we will delve into an analysis of what capital actually is. By exploring its essential qualitative characteristics, we will see how the conception of civil capital emerges from a clear understanding of those qualities.

The third point, the sufficiency of generosity, takes on a breakthrough quality—and even a spiritual sense of inspiration—because it speaks to the realistic possibility of the provenance of civil capital.

Finally, the last point examines the institutional basis for civil endowment. This too has a breakthrough quality, in that it points to the feasibility of this idea in practice. Those who feel the weight of urgency concerning humanity's present and future suffering also feel the frustration of working with existing institutions, and particularly with the unhealthy power arrangements between government and business interests. Civil society administration of civil endowments provides a very realistic way of sidestepping those conflicts.

The Primacy of Capital

The historical period since the Industrial Revolution can accurately be called an "age of capital." It is characterized by great productivity arising from technological innovation. This productivity has depended on a complex process of investment of knowledge, resources, and human effort. Historically speaking, this situation is more or less irreversible. Perhaps a few of us could go back to a very low-tech, agrarian, or even hunter-gatherer economy. But if you think about it realistically, the way forward is toward a society that uses technology in clean and skillful ways and reverses the errors of the primitive industrial age—an age from which we must emerge or face catastrophe. The key challenges that have never been addressed, and that must be addressed, are the questions of (1) how to evolve or re-establish our industrial civilization such that it does not destroy the Earth's ecosystem and, (2) how to share the benefits of the profound productivity of capital with everyone in the human family.

In economic terms, the basic idea of capital always involves some sort of productive investment. There is a provisioning of knowledge, work, and material resources with an aim toward a productive return. This is true whether you are making a stone ax by hand or building a microprocessor fabrication plant. What we call capital goods are things that are produced in order to create more production.

Of course, the definition of capital has fluctuated over time, and it has been the subject of a great deal of controversy. In the 19th century, there was a trend toward seeing capital as the physical means of production, such as factory equipment, along with wages that are advanced to pay for production. More recently, that definition has expanded to include financial investments more generally, in particular inputs in support of business ventures. According to Joseph Schumpeter's *History of Economic Analysis*, the use of the term capital to refer to money put forward for a business venture actually goes back to Roman times.[1] This is entirely appropriate, as money itself is instrumental in the economic process, and it certainly is a human invention. It is a social technology. Obviously, the operation of financial capital in practice carries tremendous pitfalls and potential for abuse. Nevertheless, it is fine to recognize the idea of financial capital, as long as we don't think that is all that capital is.

Whether capital is seen as a purposeful financial outlay, or as tangible productive equipment, we can say it is the "stuff" of investment. Investment, in turn, is a critical causal factor in a modern economy. Since capital investment is concerned with productivity, it is future focused. It is quite literally the operational process that we put in place to create the economic future. Physicist David Bohm used the term "creorder" to describe a process that simultaneously establishes something and organizes it. This is especially applicable to capital, since a specific investment always has the element of provisioning wealth to establish a particular process, a process that has a plan and design associated with it. Therefore, we can say that capital investment creorders the economy.

As complex and extensive as the global economy is, it is in a process of constant re-creation—or re-creordering—over time through investment decisions. Therefore, if we ask ourselves how to transform the economy, we could answer, "one investment at a time." That sort of answer, of course, is the sort of thinking behind socially responsible (SRI) and impact investing. With that said, it

1) Joseph A. Schumpeter, *A History of Economic Analysis* (New York: Oxford University Press, 1954), p. 322-323

CIVIL ENDOWMENT

is very important to make it clear that the civil endowment idea is fundamentally a step beyond SRI/impact investing, and we will explore in detail how that is so in the next section of this chapter.

We should also keep in mind, of course, that investment decisions can merely have the effect of recreating the economic status quo—which is in fact mostly what they do. Although this may obscure the recognition of the transformative potential of capital, we must not let it do so. We should remain alert to the real potential of capital even if most investment activity in our present-day economy tends to perpetuate unsustainable economic processes and highly unequal levels of wealth and income.

It is important to see that the transformative potential of capital acts at a qualitative level, through the ordering and re-ordering of the economic process. We will explore this process further in terms of causality in a future chapter. In brief, though, we should recognize here that capital has a central role to play in the causality of the very nature of productive and distributive processes. Capital is central in how it creates and orders specific processes, but it is also granular in the sense that it operates by way of specific investments at specific points in time. It is not inherent to the nature of investment that it need be utterly selfish; nor must leadership toward unselfish patterns of investment come from a central authority. Individual actors can make these choices, at least to the degree that we have an open society.

Once we see all this, we will see the potential—and the need—for the reformation of capital itself. Some people talk about reforming capitalism, and others talk about scrapping it and trying something else. The argument presented here can be summarized by revisiting the saying:

"Capitalism can't be reformed, but capital can."

The Conception of Civil Capital

What we've seen so far in this chapter is this: If you are genuinely concerned about the future of the planet, social justice, and economic innovation, it is crucial to develop understanding and focus on the pivotal causal significance of capital in a modern economy. That is the first aspect of the leap. Once we see that capital is a key causal factor, we should then investigate it carefully as to its essential qualities.

What *is* capital, really?

We will examine capital here in terms of three qualities: essence, nature, and manifestation. Seeing these basic characteristics of capital opens the door to seeing its full potential, including possibilities for its reformation. I will try to establish how understanding these three qualities will enable us to arrive at the conception of *civil capital*, namely, capital that is fully endowed to the universal beneficiary (all human beings now living, and those yet to be born).

It is important to start with the recognition that capital arises in some sort of context. It has a specific place, a specific time span of operation, and a specific social context. As well, and importantly for this discussion, it has a specific intention. Although it may seem paradoxical to say this, if we do not see the fact that capital is a coming together of very specific factors, we will not see what it is in general. It should be clearly understood that capital is the specific application of resources to a productive purpose. But what are those resources? By looking at what sorts of conditions and resources come together to form capital, we can advance our understanding.

Let's start with the key point as to the nature of capital, which is that it is SOCIALLY CONSTRUCTED. This is true despite the fact that individual initiative and creativity are involved. Taking the example of a handmade stone axe head, we could perhaps put forth a highly hypothetical case of an individual on a desert island, who learns by experimentation how to make an axe head, where to find the proper kind of rock, and so on. But that is an extremely unlikely case. The far more likely scenario is that the knowledge of making stone tools would be passed down through a family or clan, along with the knowledge of where to find the right kind of stone, and how to use the axe.

If we fast forward to our contemporary world, isn't this all the more so true with modern technology and finance? Isn't it true that the modern process of scientific and technological invention is a story of discovery and innovation building on itself over hundreds of years? And isn't it true that modern knowledge itself is built upon human wisdom and practical know-how stretching back into remote antiquity?

Therefore, the first main point in support of the idea that capital is socially constructed is that any sort of capital goods—and the capital process generally—contains embodied knowledge.

Capital is also socially constructed because it involves property and power relations. It depends on access to wealth, which could also be called economic power. In fact, a simple way of talking about capital is that it is about putting economic wherewithal to a productive purpose. That being so, we need to acknowledge the related fact that access to economic power is socially constructed. Access takes place through conventions and circumstances of class, race, and gender, along with generally established notions of property rights, and in keeping with the overarching political structure of a society at a given time and place. When we think of capital, we often think of the inventor, the entrepreneur, and the business enterprise. In fact, all these roles or institutions exist in a social context. The very idea of, say, investing money in a business venture is a story, a meme, that exists in our shared imagination. It has its conventions, its mythology, and its enabling conditions. Individual initiative and innovation is very much a part of the story of capital, and nothing in this description of its social nature should be construed in a way as to deny that fact.

Whether we think of the nature of capital primarily in terms of its social or individual ramifications—or, as we should, in both—we are led to the deeper question of the essence of capital. Taking our investigation to the very source, we will see that capital is in essence **mind created**. It depends ultimately on knowledge, skill, purpose, and intention. It is these psychological resources that then organize all the other factors of productivity, including financial resources, materials, energy, and human labor.

Capital can be understood in terms of its essence, nature, *and* manifestation.

All such factors are needed for economic activity, but they would be completely disorganized and ineffectual without the application of human intelligence. Now, one can argue immediately that, of course, labor involves intelligence too. This is entirely true. All that is being asserted here is that the essence of capital is a psychological one. This fact is to some extent obscured by the point we started with, namely, that it is also socially constructed. The fact that capital arises from a confluence of political power, property relations, social conventions, customs, institutions, knowledge, and creative initiative—all of which develop over time in a given society—makes it somewhat hard to see that each and every one of these social "facts" has been created and instituted by the human mind. These circumstances are definitely mind created but, because they have come

CIVIL ENDOWMENT

about in a long, historical process involving countless individuals, that fact tends to be obscured. Nevertheless, to really grasp the nature and essence of capital—and also its inherent potential—we need to penetrate to this most basic level of understanding.

To summarize so far, we can say that the essence of capital is psychological, and the nature of its construction is social.

Although capital is oriented toward the present and future, it also has historical roots. Each specific instance of capital incorporates physical resources accumulated in the past. As we have noted, it also embodies knowledge and skills that are part of the historical legacy of human knowledge, passed down from both the distant and more immediate past. This point is vitally important, in terms of recognizing the socially and mentally constructed nature of capital, and also in terms of sorting out questions of economic justice.

In this light we can immediately see, for example, why the distribution of control of capital is so highly unequal. It is obviously so because economic rights and circumstances in general have historically been highly unequal. The social construction of capital mirrors the conditions of society.

The German economist Folkert Wilken provided major insights for this line of thinking in his book *The Liberation of Capital*. Wilken (1890–1981) was a German professor who was also a deep student of the work of Rudolf Steiner. It should be mentioned from the start here that Wilken does not make "the leap" in this book and arrive at a conception of civil capital. What he does do, however, is to deepen the conversation about capital in a unique way and provide a great deal of grounding from within the history of economic reasoning, all of which is of very helpful significance to civil endowment theory.

Wilken expressed the psychological nature of capital with the phrase, "the origin of capital in *geist*."[2]

Geist is a German term that the translator of *The Liberation of Capital* left in the original German, simply because there is no one English term that fully carries its implications. It is often translated as "spirit," a word that in turn has multiple meanings in English. The meaning that comes closest to its use in the present context can be seen in the phrase, "the spirit of friendship."

Just to make it clear that I'm not talking about a particular spirit here, but rather how the term is used, I will put forth an opposite sort of phrase, "the spirit of war," which uses the term in the same way. "Spirit" does not refer to some sort of entity, nor is it meant as something religious or "spiritual." In this context, the meaning used for geist/spirit is "a psychological stance, an intention, or purpose." The key point here is that capital has geist. It has a particular psychological content and mentality. In *Capitalism 3.0*, Peter Barnes uses the evocative metaphor of an "operating system."[3]

In the most general sense, we can say that the spirit or geist of capital is the intention of productivity. We can call this the pervasive intention. The exact nature of the process behind the productivity of capital is highly specific to any particular investment. This can be called the operational plan. As well, there is also a more general spirit, an underlying basis or attitude within the psychological framework of capital. This foundational spirit has more to do with the overarching philosophy of the productive process than with the details of the process itself. It speaks to the human values behind the investment—or, for that matter, the indifference

---

2) Folkert Wilken, *The Liberation of Capital* (London: George Allen and Unwin, 1982) p. 5

3) Peter Barnes, *Capitalism 3.0* (San Francisco: Berrett-Koehler Publishers, 2006)

to such values. If we penetrate this fundamental geist, this fundamental spirit, we will begin to see an inherent flexibility of structure that enables the conception of civil capital to emerge.

Keeping in mind that capital includes the historical legacy of shared knowledge passed down to us in human culture, we can now summarize the types of psychological content of capital in terms of four aspects. These are: embedded knowledge, pervasive intention, operating plan, and foundational spirit.

EMBEDDED KNOWLEDGE is the aforementioned shared stream of skill and wisdom from the distant and immediate past that is inevitably accessed in the operation of capital. The PERVASIVE INTENTION is simply the conscious allocation of resources to a productive purpose. It underlies the very conception of capital, whether those purposes are good or bad, skillful or unskillful, successful or not successful. The OPERATING PLAN consists of the concrete business plan and circumstances of the investment. It is the psychological content of how the basic idea of productive investment is instantiated. Finally, the FOUNDATIONAL SPIRIT is the fundamental stance that stands between the pervasive intention and the operational plan.

This last aspect of the essence of capital is often ignored or over generalized. It is often assumed, for example, that the foundational spirit is merely the will to profit maximization, or to gaining and maintaining socio-political power.[4]

Certainly there is reason in today's world to see things this way, but to see such attitudes as inherent to capital is a mistake.

With this in mind, let's look a little closer at the idea of founda-

---

4) Shimshon Bichler and Jonathan Nitzan, Capital as Power: Toward a New Cosmology of Capitalism (real-world economics review, online issue no. 61, 2012)

tional spirit. The key point for the present discussion is to see the operation of this foundational spirit, and point out how that spirit, for better or worse, is embedded in the functioning of capital. It is essential to recognize this spirit as a part of the overall capital geist, since this is where the creative possibilities lie. The foundational spirit is the overall intention and philosophy of investment. It includes, most importantly, our ethical attitudes and aspirations. The reductionist, atomistic mentality of modern economics has tended to reduce this spirit to a machine-like attitude of profit maximization. The tendency that is at work is to turn an observed general case into a universal case, and to make theoretical assumptions based on that. However, it is crucial at this point in our reasoning to *not* assume that this is the exclusive case. In fact, the now-widespread practices of socially responsible and impact investing disprove the notion that investing is—or need be—purely about profit and power. This discussion has been quite abstract, so let's step back here and look at some examples.

We could start with a somewhat stereotyped business idea of a 19th century capitalist—but one that is not very far from the historical truth. He might plan to build a factory by purchasing a building and some weaving equipment, and hire people to make some kind of product. Behind this plan is the pervasive intention, namely, to allocate resources to some kind of productivity. The specifics of the enterprise make up the operational plan. We can also imagine that he would hire lower-class workers and pay them the absolute minimum, starvation wages, force them to work long hours under terrible working conditions, and make as much money as possible for himself by selling the products. The human values behind this exploitive, extractive approach would be the foundational spirit in this case.

Conventionally, we would regard the capital here as the weaving equipment and wages, or more generally as the wealth that was put forth to finance the venture altogether. In Wilken's expanded definition of the concept, capital includes socially created economic power along with the specific plan, spirit, or idea of a venture. What could be called the tangible capital, be it the factory equipment or the particular financial arrangements, simply cannot be separated out from underlying social and psychological factors. Indeed, the tangible manifestations of capital are direct manifestations and reflections of the factors that made them possible.

Of course, we could just as well talk about a more modern example of a capitalist who planned to buy some high-tech equipment, hire and train well-paid and well-treated workers, and make a product that was good for the environment with "triple-bottom-line" motivation. That too would be an example of the operation of the various kinds of spirit or geist in an application of capital.

It is clear that beneath the particulars of a specific manifestation of capital are certain very basic assumptions or intentions that form its foundational spirit. These may in fact be unconscious or unexamined assumptions, in the sense that they simply follow social convention. But they are still there. These factors can be expressed as qualitative dimensions of capital, as depicted in the illustrations on pages 84 and 85. They can also be expressed conceptually as answers to the following questions:

For whom is this capital allocated? This is usually expressed as a question of who gets the profit. But we must also ask who is expected to handle the ancillary outcomes, such as social and environmental effects. These are usually called "externalities" by businesses, a term which neatly expresses the typical attitude toward such outcomes. But a fully inclusive analysis of such things would not, needless to say, treat them in that way. To put it precisely: what individual or group are the overall effects (including productivity and profit) of this investment meant for?

On what time scale is this investment made?

What is the ethical stance of the production process and the product itself? This question also pertains to the question of externalities, the effects that ripple out from the production process.

Qualitative Continua in Capital Investment

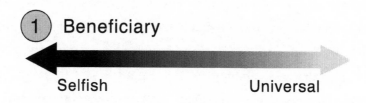

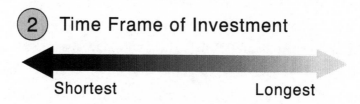

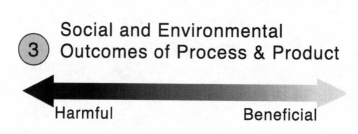

These three continua could be called "dimensions" or "continua" of the foundational spirit of capital. If we take each of them to the upper extreme (here expressed on the right side of the illustration), we arrive at civil capital.

Taking these dimensions of the foundational geist to their logical extremes, we see how certain things converge. If we are designating the beneficiary as universal, we automatically need to work on the furthest possible timeline. Not only that, we also have to optimize the ethical dimension of production, simply because there is no one to exploit, no possibility of burdening future generations, and no excuse for externalizing negative outcomes. Thus, although these three types of consideration have been pointed out individually here, they are by no means independent variables.

Thus, by asking these questions and examining the graph of the qualitative continua, the civil capital idea emerges. By taking the dimensions of beneficiary and time frame to their end points, we see a notion of a universal beneficiary and an unbounded time frame.

Integrated View: The Convergence of the Continua

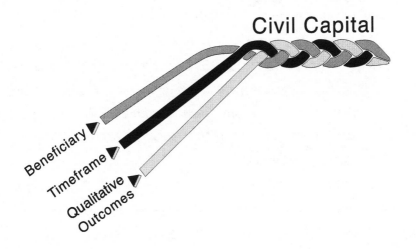

In other words, by seeing capital in terms of the full range of possible intentions, it becomes abundantly clear that there could be capital for the common good and the indefinite future. Connected with that, we will see a particular ethical orientation toward ripple-out effects that logically follows from that stance. Clearly, such capital cannot be exploitive, extractive, or externalizing; or, to put it more practically, these characteristics need to be minimized.

On the basis of these considerations, we can point out some general examples of the governing spirit of capital. They could be called machine spirit, mammalian spirit, and finally, the spirit of civil capital.

Machine spirit refers to capital that operates automatically, with a complete lack of moral or human sensibility. It is simply concerned with replicating and increasing itself according to the single bottom line. It is utterly unconcerned with human or qualitative considerations.

This imagery accords with early, Newtonian conceptions of an economy that operates according to completely impersonal forces, ruled by universal laws. This machine-like conception of the economy, of course, lives on in the orthodox economic dogma of our day. It expresses itself in a wholly mathematical, quantitative conception of economic benefit, and in the general conceptions of the rational maximizer, the profit maximizing corporation, the doctrine of strategic economic advantage among countries, and so on. Machine capital reaches its logical culmination when the wealth of powerful holders of capital enables them to seize the political apparatus of a society. And this of course is the phase we are in today. Machine capital could also be described in more colorful terms, such as "zombie capital," "reptilian capital," and so on.

Mammalian capital brings in a higher level of human concerns. It is "warm-blooded." It is what underlies what has traditionally been considered to be the ethical practice of doing business. Socially responsible investing creates this kind of capital. Mammalian capital does not challenge basic ideas of private ownership. It simply tries to exercise that ownership in more positive ways, especially in terms of environmental and social effects.

Finally, we can consider the spirit of civil capital. As we have seen, if we look at capital, not from the point of view of how it is conventionally conceived, but from the perspective of its nature and essence—and hence its possibilities—and we look at the details of the qualitative range of those possibilities (the continua), civil capital will pop out

Capital for the common good. What could be simpler?

as an clear, logical conclusion to the investigation. It is good that it's obvious! Capital for the common good. What could be simpler? Interestingly enough, I believe you will find the conception of civil capital to be both logical *and* intuitive in nature.

Civil capital is simply the culmination of the possibilities that were there all along. Therefore, we can now define the spirit or geist of civil capital. It is to benefit the universal beneficiary on an unbounded timeline. Unbiased compassion is the foundation of this spirit. It is the outcome of post-materialist and co-centric analysis applied to an understanding of the central importance of capital in a modern economy.

I believe there is some meaning and value in calling civil capital "the perfection of capital." However, I am not using this terminology in some wild, utopian way. We can talk about perfection here in the same way that the mathematical idea of a circle is perfect, even though it is impossible to create a perfect circle in the physical world. I would argue that such usage is not utopian in the sense that we are merely referring to the culmination of an idea.

Now that we have a perspective on the psychological essence and social nature of capital, we can consider its manifestation—power. In particular, this refers to productive power—the capability to make an economically useful product. It is important to distinguish socio-political power from economically productive power, although of course they are related. Indeed, socio-political power is involved in almost all cases as a condition for the allocation of the resources that come together in capital formation. And, as we see in a very stark way in the contemporary world, the concentration of wealth that can arise from productivity translates very easily to political forms of power.

Nevertheless, to see things clearly, we should contemplate the idea of purely economic productive power, in part as a matter of theoretical rigor, but perhaps more importantly, because it enables us—in the context of civil capital—to envision a complete transformation of the application of that power. If capital is power, and if the beneficiary of that power could be the universal beneficiary, there is a very striking conclusion that can be drawn, namely, that there is a possibility of universal access to economic wellbeing in open society, based on the egalitarian provisioning and subsequent productivity of civil capital.

The manifestation of capital is economic power.

A second, ancillary type of outcome of the power of civil capital is the potential for gains in social and political justice that could arise from more widespread economic empowerment and wellbeing. I do believe, for example, that the presence of civil endowments will strengthen the conditions for open society. However, trying to translate economic strength into political power is a risky business at best, and I believe that the movement, as it evolves, will be far better served by maintaining a very indirect involvement with politics, in keeping with its civil society character.

In conclusion, it should be mentioned that for me the basic idea of civil endowment evolved, not from some permutation of the existing theory of capital, but from an extended contemplation at a pragmatic level as to what is needed and what is possible. I saw that what is needed is a pattern of investment that provides for economic wellbeing on an egalitarian basis, and that simultaneously moves and transforms the economy in an environmentally sustainable direction. Therefore, whatever contribution this system of thought may be to capital theory is an outgrowth of a design challenge that demanded a practical response. Nevertheless, I think it is incredibly important to investigate and reconsider capital at a fundamental theoretical level, because what emerges from that analysis is the understanding that the formation of civil capital is not only possible, but it is also a reasonable, worthy, and just innovation for our contemporary economy.

The Sufficiency of Generosity

We now turn to the third aspect of "the leap," which speaks to the feasibility of this whole idea. Just as we don't need to base our assumptions about the governing spirit of capital on the general observed case, we do not need to base our ideas on the source of capital on such conventions. Marx, it will be remembered, viewed capital as arising from surplus value that is stolen from the workers. The neoclassical view would be that capital arises from retained earnings in the production process and, more generally speaking, from savings. These two views are not very far apart, aside from the part about it being stolen! In any case, aside from the other similarities of these views, they are also similar in that they make generalizations based on what is generally observed to be so and ignore other possibilities as unimportant. In that sense, they are both conservative, conventional views.

If we have really understood, though, the psychological basis of capital formation, we will see that absolutely any source of wealth can be deployed as capital. In fact, one conventional source of capital— namely, inheritance—is in effect a gift that is commonly employed as such. The whole idea that generosity could be the source of wealth for civil capital is an outgrowth of this basic idea, which we could call "open provenance." The wealth can come from anywhere, and in any way. It could be a $20-dollar bill that washes up on a beach.[5]

The generosity that creates civil capital is the psychological act of endowing it to the universal beneficiary.

What is seen in this dimension of the leap is that generosity is adequate as a source for civil capital. To realize that this is so, we have to consider that, at the onset, we are not claiming we can change the overall economic system at its full scale, or on a rapid time schedule. What is claimed, and what is truly possible, is that we can establish a seed of civil endowment, and that doing so is transformational at any scale.

---

5) Some years ago, when I first described the idea of civil endowment to my friend Deborah Bansemer, she went in a back room and came out and handed me a $20 dollar bill, which she explained she had found washed up on a beach in Florida. She said she was saving it for "a really special purpose." Thanks, Deb.

Of course, the proposed system of endowments is one that can scale up very easily, by way of the establishment of countless endowments everywhere in the world, all of which would be mutually supportive and reinforcing, though operating under decentralized governance. However, these points are not as important initially as the insight that the actual feeling of generosity towards the whole of humanity is the seed of it all.

When we change our stance from confrontation and blame and really choose responsibility in a personal and tangible way, that is the moment that we are willing to give something—anything—that we are able to give. That is the moment in which the symbolic act of giving to any degree becomes transformative. And that is when we understand that the very feeling of generosity to the universal beneficiary is itself transformative. The transformation of economic power resides in this act of generosity. To see this is also to see that the whole process of forming civil capital and building civil endowments is valid and worthwhile *at any level of scale*. That includes putting a penny in a paper cup on a shelf and saying, "this is for civil endowment." That is the leap.

A feeling of generosity toward this particular cause of healing the world economy is a coming together of natural generosity—which we all possess—with an understanding of civil endowment. That is why this part of the leap comes after the part that understands "capital for the common good." I don't think there is a need for such understanding to be extremely nuanced. It could be just the idea that we are creating a permanent fund to be invested for all humanity. We don't have to believe that this feeling of generosity or one small act of generosity toward civil endowment will take on and conquer the juggernaut of global capitalism, the leviathan of state power—or, for that matter, the edifice of human ignorance. It is merely the recognition that, "this is transformative." It bears repeating that it is transformative of economic power. More personally, though, it is transformative of the giver. This aspect of the leap is quite individual in that sense.

With this transformative gift, there is the creation of a specific instance of civil capital. We can say that this gift is adequate in a very specific sense. It is adequate in that the potential for transformation that inspires the gift has been accomplished within that very gift. It has become tangible.

As we will see in subsequent chapters, the provenance of civil capital is by no means limited to simple gifts by individuals—if that were the case, the whole idea would not be a particularly practical one, although it still would have the symbolic power of inner transformation described above.

When we get to the prospects of structuralized generosity, especially those arising from the productivity of civil capital itself, there are real possibilities for the development of endowments large enough to really change things in fundamental ways in society. That is very exciting, as long as we remember that generosity still will be the fundamental motivating force behind whatever structures and norms we create to channel resources into those endowments.

The Civil Mandate

Even if we have appreciated the first three aspects of the leap, it is natural to ask how civil endowments would be governed and managed. Indeed, this is a make-or-break question in terms of feasibility of the whole idea. The last segment of the leap is to see that the stewardship and governance of civil endowments will come neither from government nor from the business community. It will come from civil society. Civil endowment theory does not depend on eliminating or changing the basic nature of individual self-interest, private property, the business firm, or the political process. Although changes are needed in all these areas, we must accept that such changes will take place incrementally and within their own specific context. Civil endowment theory concerns itself with civil society guidance and leadership and, most significantly, with *civil society economic power.*

This possibility of civil society guidance, influence, and power in the economy is a key component of the civil endowment idea. This is not a political solution, nor is it intended to be

Stewardship of civil endowments will come from civil society.

controlled or guided by the private economy. Thus, the structural design for implementation of civil endowment is part of a more general possibility, that of a civil-guided economy altogether. The roots of such a direction are very much in place today, in the form of the immensely diverse and extensive network of non-profits, NGOs, ad hoc advocacy groups, and traditional institutions such as educational and spiritual groups that exist worldwide. Civil society power and influence are also seen in longstanding economic forms such as labor unions, cooperatives, worker-owned businesses, credit unions, and land trusts. There is no reason that non-profit organizations cannot be specifically designed and chartered to administer civil endowments.

Although that is so, we cannot ignore the social and political conditions that exist in various parts of the world. Many countries do not have the degree of open society necessary for civil endowments to take root. In most general terms, "open society" means a system in which there are basic political and economic rights and freedoms, fundamental legal justice, and the rights of institutions other than government to function.

Although these conditions obviously do not exist everywhere, there are several mitigating considerations in that regard. First, some degree of open society exists pretty much everywhere, especially through the internet and global communications generally, even if it is "under the radar." The desire for the qualities of an open society is universal to the human spirit, and that desire is only enhanced by the knowledge that it exists, even if somewhere else. Second, the investments that civil endowments make will benefit people in all parts of the world, even if those investments cannot be made directly in certain areas due to political conditions. An example of this is any investment that mitigates climate change. As well, it may be possible for civil endowments to make investments in places where non-profits cannot operate freely, simply because the for-profit realm has a lot of freedom to operate in today's world. This is true even in places where open society is quite restricted.

Just as a civil endowment system depends on open society, it can also be an influence for the enhancement and preservation of open society. It could help open society emerge in places that do not currently have it, and it could help open society flourish in areas that do have it. This is so simply because civil endowment is a force for economic and social justice—which are the very defining characteristics of open society.

We should note here that global capitalism as currently practiced, with its amoral quest for profits, is *not* a force for open society. We see that fact not only in the transition from communism to capitalism in Russia and China, but also in trends in the United States and Europe—and certainly in the developing world. Thus, although civil endowment is emphatically not proposed as a political movement, it carries the distinct possibility of fostering positive change in the political circumstances of humanity.

The fact that a civil endowment system does not require any sort of fundamental political reform or legislation to get started is an essential aspect of its feasibility. Isn't it true that so many positive and progressive ideas and movements are in effect spinning their wheels, all due to the fact that they cling to the notion of political solutions—solutions that are far easier to derail than they are to implement? The degree of reactionary obstructionism that is present in politics here in the United States is perhaps more extreme than in Europe, but Europe seems to be following suit. The situation worldwide, although mixed, is hardly better.

The stubborn fact is that positive political reform is a slow, messy, uncertain process. And on top of this fact, the overarching reality is that political administration of an economy, even with the best of intentions, has fundamental flaws and limitations. Usually, of course, that argument is advanced to support the interests of the private sector in the form of so-called *laissez faire* or privatization, which effectively supports the global capitalist system. History has shown, however, that hegemony of *either* sector, governmental or private, over the economy is fatally flawed. The third option—that of a civil-guided economy—is not some sort of last resort. In fact, it is a very elegant solution—along with being an urgently needed change in direction.

We will extensively explore the details of how governance institutions for civil endowment can be structured in a later chapter, "The Special Proposal."

In summary, here is what we could obtain from the four aspects of the leap:

1. RECOGNITION of the central importance of capital

2. An UNDERSTANDING of the civil-capital concept

3. INSPIRATION as to the sufficiency of generosity in seeding civil capital

4. REALIZATION that a civil endowment system is possible through decentralized civil-society governance

This chapter may seem a bit long for a leap! However, the leap doesn't necessarily come from reading this material, but more from reflecting on it and allowing intuition and logical thought processes to work together. The leap came to me through persistently contemplating an economic design challenge, a search for fundamental solutions to the human predicament of our times.

The Case for Civil Endowment

IN THE PREVIOUS CHAPTER, WE LOOKED AT THE INSIGHTS THAT make up the key ideas of civil endowment. They are the conceptual underpinnings needed to understand this proposed structural innovation, which could realistically be created in our contemporary world society, starting now. In this chapter, I will develop reasoning that explains why we could and should do just that. We will look at it from three points of view: those of compassion, justice, and causality. I consider the reasoning from compassion to be ultimately most compelling, but this does not mean the other arguments are unimportant. It would scarcely be compassionate to build a system that was not an expression of justice, and it would certainly be unwise to build one that had no chance of working as intended. Therefore, the three sets of reasoning are all essential.

The Reasoning from Compassion

As has been mentioned, although we are concerned with compassion in this book, the emphasis is not on getting you to give rise to it in a general way. I certainly encourage that, but I believe you have plenty of it already. What this section in particular *is* about, though, is connecting your compassion with the idea of civil endowment. It is to make the point that civil endowment is a useful and effective way to apply compassion to our contemporary world situation.

The six economic virtues have obviously been with us a long time, as have their expressions in conventional charity and philanthropy. That is a very good thing, and nothing here is meant to criticize the many expressions of those virtues that are so important in our world. This discussion is merely meant to add a new area of focus. We should keep in mind in this discussion that we are using the idea of compassion here not only to refer to the wish to remove the suffering of others, but in an expanded sense that includes the full range of positive possibilities for human beings and for civilization.

The reasoning presented here is meant to promote an understanding that such compassion is a valid basis for creating a civil endowment system. This will be presented in three main points: 1) that reasoning from basic human values is appropriate in economics; 2) that compassion in particular is a valid—and in fact central—human value for such reasoning; and, 3) that compassion is the most compelling and effective argument for civil endowment.

As has been mentioned, the arguments from the point of view of justice and causality are also essential parts of the overall case to be made, but compassion (and compassion as inseparable from wisdom) is the underlying basis for those other arguments. Compassion is also the easiest rationalization to understand and, if understood, provides a very effective tipping point in terms of motivation. It is fine to accept an idea intellectually, but will we actually work for it? If anything will make us work for it, it will be compassion.

Starting with the first point, we should recall that conventional economics—and its dominant neoclassical branch in particular—is still in the grip of 18th and 19th century science, which viewed life and nature in atomistic and mechanistic ways. Human motivations are reduced to simple self-interest. The human mind is accepted as being part of the system, but only in very narrow ways. Therefore, although it may seem absurd to a contemporary reader, it is still worth making the point that economics is a social discipline, and that positive human values are appropriate starting points for deliberations.

We are at a point in history where a very significant proportion of people worldwide realize that human beings have motivations other than simple greed, and that the human race is part of a whole system, one that includes not only all of humanity, but also the planetary ecosystem. An implication of recognizing the whole-system character of the economy, and our own inseparability from it, is what His Holiness the Dalai Lama calls "universal responsibility." At the United Nations Conference on Environment and Development (UNCED) held in Rio de Janeiro in 1992, His Holiness said:

> I believe that to meet the challenge of our times, human beings will have to develop a greater sense of universal responsibility. Each of us must learn to work not for his or her self, family or nation, but for the benefit of all mankind. Universal responsibility is the real key to human survival. It is the best foundation for world peace, the equitable use of natural resources and through concern for the future generations, the proper care of the environment.

In a very real sense, the inner dimension of actually stepping up to our universal responsibility and forming the aspiration to work for the wellbeing of the whole of humanity is a heart-level experience of compassion. It is a feeling that extends toward all the individuals with whom we share this world—for their suffering, their hopes and fears, and their potential. This attitude creates the possibility for healing at the whole system level. Compassion is the subjective experience of connection and interrelatedness. Since knowing (and feeling) connection and interrelatedness are expressions of wisdom, we can say that compassion is a valid human value on which to base our reasoning and our actions. But what are the tangible steps to put it into practice?

This is where we can make a connection between our feeling of whole-system compassion and the whole-system remedy of civil endowment. To be sure, there are countless ways to practice universal responsibility. This discussion is not meant to depreciate any of them, but it *is* meant to point out civil endowment as one of those ways.

The first step in this undertaking of universal responsibility based on compassion is something that happens at the mind level—first, within ourselves, and then as we model it for others. For that reason—and although civil endowment is definitely designed as a tangible application of economic capital—we cannot discount, especially in its early stages, its efficacy purely as an idea. The mere existence of endowments for all humanity will have an effect on the minds of those who hear of them.

This could be called "positive reflexivity." George Soros has written about the idea of reflexivity in financial markets, wherein the psychological expectations of market players become a factor in the actual movement of markets.[1]

The concept of reflexivity can be applied in a general way to civil endowment.

We all know that acts of kindness spur other such acts. Shared belief in trusting relationships is self-fulfilling in many ways.

---

1) George Soros, *The Alchemy of Finance: Reading the Mind of the Market* (New York: John Wiley & Sons, Inc., 1987) p. 27-81

Establishing, even at a small level, bodies of capital dedicated to universal compassion and responsibility will have definite effect on the optimism, confidence, and sense of possibility that people feel. It is important to see this symbolic effect, since otherwise it might be hard to believe that our preliminary efforts to establish civil endowments might be too small to make a difference.

I think a lot of people can get the idea of civil endowment directly and intuitively through this reasoning from compassion. They might respond to the idea with, "Yes, that makes sense. A certain share goes to the common good, to be invested for present and future generations. What's so difficult about that?" Thus, the reasoning from compassion is ultimately the most convincing and effective—and that can be true even for people who do engage with and understand the more elaborate arguments.

Civil endowments will engender "positive reflexivity."

For example, compassion can smooth over the uncertainties as to details of valid claims made in the argument from justice, such as, "What is the rightful share of capital profits for the universal beneficiary?" It replaces such questions with ones about generosity like, "What are we willing to give here?" or, "How much can we give without hardship or disruption?" Compassion can also smooth over the uncertainty about whether a civil endowment system will work in practice based on arguments from causality. Compassion says, "OK, give it a try on a small scale and see where that goes."

Compassion also cuts through social barriers to implementing civil endowments. Imagine trying to enact a law (and, by the way, in what government or jurisdiction would such a law take effect?)

that stipulates that some percentage of transactions or profits or natural resources goes to the universal beneficiary. It would be *very* difficult to make that happen. Even if it were possible, and people were compelled to contribute in that way through the force of law, they would resent it, just as they resent taxes. There would be no end to the reaction to it all—and no end to complaining, obstruction, and negative feelings. By contrast, if civil endowments are established through voluntary contributions—from generosity arising from compassion—the exact opposite will be true.

Finally, compassion will give us the courage to take the risk to practice social innovation in this way. We will see that this is not some sort of abstract intellectual game. It is a serious endeavor to relieve suffering and foster human potential, now and in the future. Compassion creates a very strong motivation to change the circumstances and prospects for the very poor, the yet unborn, and for civilization itself.

This is why compassion is the first and foremost key to civil endowment. It is a deciding force, one that is transformative and motivating. To make it so, we need to enhance our natural compassion, let ourselves be transformed by it, and then work to put it into action. This is the possibility that reveals itself in the full conception of civil endowment.

Reasoning Based on Justice

Let us begin by reflecting on the issue of economic justice from the points of view of the past, present and future. Illogically, perhaps, we will start with the future. We will do so because capital investment generally is future oriented. It involves creating the conditions for productivity. The civil endowment idea, with its emphasis on a universal beneficiary that includes all future generations, is specifically designed to create not only the conditions for productivity in the future, but the conditions for economic justice as well. Clearly, a key rationale for creating civil endowments now is that they are needed for the future. In light of what we now know about, say, climate change, the whole notion that we could exclude people yet to be born from our conception of justice seems ridiculously inadequate—a sort of ethical flatland.

This, of course, has been a key theme of the sustainability and environmental movements in general: to convince us to take the future seriously, and in particular to think about how our present day actions impact coming generations. In many ways, although these movements have correctly pointed out many of the kinds of changes that need to be made, they have largely done so without envisioning needed innovations in economic practice. If we are willing to imagine the horrific conditions and suffering associated with extreme climate change, and the associated radical challenges to civilization itself, we ought to be willing to think radically in terms of new initiatives such as civil endowment. For me, the only thing that makes optimism possible is being able to face squarely the question of justice for future members of the human family, and being willing to take action that is as decisive as the situation demands.

This leads us directly to considerations of the present, because it is clear that we have an ethical obligation to act in the present in ways that provide for justice in the future. The present, as we know, is where we actually live, and where we have the capability of doing things. Even more to the point, it is where we have the chance to *change our way* of doing things.

Seen with honest eyes, the state of our world today is very troubling. Of course, there are islands of progress and genuine trends for the good. Our urge to activism is often focused on very specific issues, which of course is needed. But there is equally a need to implement justice at the most systemic level possible. The case I make for civil endowment is that it is a pervasive, system-changing implementation of economic justice. It is not about fixing specific issues, important as that is. We can begin working for this new era of systemic justice right now. Isn't it true that a new future is beginning in every moment? Seeing things in that way gives us access to the radical recognition of freedom that comes from being truly present.

Still, we must also understand the legacy of the past. In particular, and despite the fact that it is hard to even think about such things, we have to consider the immensity of the injustice we humans have inflicted on each other over the span of history. How will we move forward from the legacy of pain and suffering that has come about from violence, war, annexation, genocide, enslavement, expropriation, and exploitation? Although these types of events are not entirely economic in nature, clearly they all have an economic component. Therefore, if we include—as we should—all such horrors in our thinking, we will see that the enormity and vastness of the economic injustice inflicted in the past. This injustice carries forward into the ongoing injustice of our world in the present.

Is atonement and healing possible? We will explore this question in depth in a coming chapter, but I will say here that, if done with the correct mental attitude, the work of building a civil endowment system and providing resources for it can actually serve as a process of atonement for the past, and work as a force for restorative justice.

When we think about justice in terms of economic theory, it should be remembered that the predominant streams of economic thought—modes of thinking that are deeply engrained in people's thinking—have definite things to say about economic justice. The capitalist mode of thinking sees justice in individual rights. The socialist mode of thinking sees justice in the power of the state to establish a fair and inclusive economy through collective ownership. Modern liberal democracy (which in Europe would be called social democracy) is something of a blend of these views, emphasizing a strong role for the state in working for economic wellbeing of all, without advocating state ownership of productive enterprises.

The problem with any and all of these systems, of course, is that they have not worked in practice. Ideologues will always argue that, "well, the free-market system has not been really free enough," or, "socialism was never complete enough." I argue a more fundamental point: that these lines of thought are fundamentally flawed and can never result in a just economic system in practice.

The picture with modern liberal democratic economics is not so black and white, of course. It could be argued that the failure of Keynesian economics to establish and maintain a smoothly running capitalist economy is more a failure of politics than of economic theory, per se. Still, failure it is.

In the present-day United States, the fact that our democratic apparatus has been by and large seized by moneyed interests represents a fundamental corruption of the possibility of just—or even sane—oversight and influence of the economy by the government. This type of problem exists in a very pronounced way worldwide. There is either a strong hegemony of political power (as in contemporary Russia), or of financial power pulling the strings of political power. In both cases, there is a collusion of financial and political interests, to the detriment of justice.

All this is to lay the ground for the statement that a civil endowment system is a categorically different approach to working for and establishing economic justice than what is represented by the established theory and practice on the subject. It seeks to reform capital, not capitalism, and to provision an adequate portion of power to civil society, one sufficient to create a working structural balance to remedy the existing unhealthy relationships between state and private interests. A civil endowment system would confer beneficial ownership of productive resources on each and every human being, now, and in the future. Furthermore, it would honor the whole-system nature of our interrelated economy, without falling into the structural defects of a centralized, planned economy under state control.

At this point, we could ask what might be seen as purely a rhetorical question—but one still worth discussing: Do we really believe that everyone deserves a place at the table? It is interesting that those who hold views on economic justice that are both right and left of center would tend to say "yes," but with different specifics. A right-of-center view would tend to focus on universal economic rights and freedoms, and a leftist view would look to economic benefits being delivered in practice to everyone through collective organization. The point is that almost anyone with any principles at all would agree that everyone should have some kind of seat at the table. But in practice, the historical outcomes of economic systems have been extremely unfair. Everyone has not gotten an equal opportunity—or, in many cases, any opportunity at all.

History did not start out with a level playing field, nor has the process of history itself ever been fair. It is important not to underestimate the entrenchment and momentum of injustice on the world level, but it is even more important not to assume that no fundamental remedies are conceivable. Civil endowment is proposed as just such a fundamental remedy.

If civil endowment is understood for what it is, it is quite easy to understand its potential as a force for universal economic justice. A civil endowment is a body of capital that is fully and equally endowed to everyone, without exception. Equality and fairness are in its very structure and intent.

What follows in this section is a deeper exploration of the question as to why it is justified for the universal beneficiary to actually *receive* a share of the wealth of humanity. In other words, we may accept that everyone should have a share in the productive assets and output of the economy, but what justifies having the universal beneficiary receive a portion of tangible assets to be aggregated as capital on an ongoing basis?

Now, this may seem like a hair-splitting exercise. If it is justified to have something, it must be justified to get it. That is true, but it still involves a transfer of wealth from some party to another. Thus, the question of justice in the delivery of wealth to the universal beneficiary is a significant one. Should we just build the endowments as a matter of charity, because it seems like a good idea? Or, does the universal beneficiary actually deserve, by right, to receive a share of the wealth of humanity?

The discussion that follows takes the viewpoint of an affirmative answer to the second question. I will try to make the case that the universal beneficiary has a valid—although partial—claim on (1) profits and productivity arising from capital investment generally; (2) natural resources; and, (3) intellectual property.

It must be emphasized that these claims are partial and could be extremely small. The point of the reasoning here is not to determine the size of the claim at all, but simply to point out that it exists. It does not exclude any conventional claimants, such as workers, suppliers of financial capital, and so on. Nor is this argument intended to suggest that the claim should be satisfied through any kind of involuntary appropriation, such as taxation. The intent of the argument is simply to establish the reasoning for a valid and rightful claim for the universal beneficiary.

Profits and Productivity Arising from Capital

The topic of social justice with regard to capital and its productivity leads us into the thick of the highly charged debates and divisions that have been going on for the better part of two centuries. The historically intractable split between left and right viewpoints on the economy hinges on precisely on this question.

In practical terms, there is also the fact that people who oppose capitalism in its modern form have little interest in capital as an economic concept, and focus on political remedies for economic problems. Those who do see and accept the power of capital mostly understand it—and use it—as an instrument for selfish purposes. Of course, in the middle are those engaged with socially responsible investment, impact investing, and the like. These views, which emerged around the 1980s, are a step forward, but represent only a partial rethinking of the capital concept. Historically speaking, the aforementioned radical polarization of views on capital has pretty much deadened the discussion at a fundamental level. This is certainly true within the economics profession.

Let us start afresh, then, and consider what justice might look like when considered from the points of view of manifestation, nature, and essence of capital, as described in the previous chapter.

In terms of manifestation, we have said that it is power. This power is not just the ability to obtain wealth and productivity, but also to determine the very nature and course of investment. We can stop right here and assert that it is only fair that everyone get some of that power. This means that everyone has the right to be considered in the structuring and operation of the economy. This right applies to future individuals as well. Civil endowments, in their capacity of working for the benefit of the most distant conceivable future, can function as something of an "ombudsman for the unborn," as it were.

In terms of the nature of capital, which is its social construction, it is strikingly obvious that the exercise of fairness and justice means universal access to the benefits of capital. Economic institutions need to be structured to embody the goals of universal sufficiency and opportunity, and to channel investment in the direction of the common good. Economic conventions—and the very structure of capital itself—are created by human decisions and actions. It follows that we could structure them in just ways.

Finally, the essence of capital is its spirit, and at the deepest level, the spirit of civil capital is the compassionate, unbiased aspiration for the wellbeing of all humanity. It is in this spirit that the seeds of the enactment of justice reside, and from which radiates its tangible nature in socially created forms, and its manifestations in beneficial power.

As we discussed in *The Leap*, pointing out that capital is ultimately psychological in essence is the first of what I consider to be Folkert Wilken's important contributions to capital theory. The second is his careful contemplation of the issues surrounding the profit that is generated by capital, which we can describe as the sum of money generated above and beyond all costs of production, including the cost of finance capital, materials, and labor. Marx, it will be remembered, saw the profits made by the capitalist as essentially stolen from the workers, since he believed in the labor theory of value. In conventional capitalist thinking, the profit or "free capital" is most definitely assumed to be the property of the capitalist, in both moral and legal terms. Wilken questioned both the Marxian and the conventional capitalist assumptions. He disagreed with the Marxian position because the productivity or value created by production cannot be assumed to come from labor only. It comes, at least in part, from psychological factors. This includes all four of the types of capital "geist," namely: embedded cultural knowledge, pervasive intention, operating plan, and foundational spirit.

In a particular case, say of a basic factory making material goods, the design and manufacture of the equipment embodies knowledge and skill of many human beings, and each of them can be said to have a claim on its productivity. If taken to its logical conclusion, however, this line of thinking also refutes the basic capitalist position on the ownership of profit. Why is that so? *It is so because no one person can really "own" the shared knowledge base of the human race.* It may be true, of course, that a particular engineer designed a particular piece of equipment. But, obviously, he or she did not invent all the technology that made that design possible.

Of course, it can be argued that the investors and entrepreneurs behind a particular venture have contributed very significant resources, in terms of time, money, or creativity. This is a valid argument, and points to the fact that they are stakeholders to the venture—as, of course, are workers generally. But the foregoing argument makes it impossible to assert that any of these groups are exclusive stakeholders.

This is the point that Wilken developed. Although he rejected the Marxian view, he did not conclude that the capitalist should have the sole claim on profit. His view was not an attack on private property in any general sense, but it did call into question the exclusivity of ownership of the profits arising from capital investment. The basic reasoning behind this point is that investment and the productive process cannot be separated out from a more universal process. Wilken concluded that profit should be rightfully understood as "wealth in trust." Wilken reached different conclusions than my own about the disposition of this wealth in trust. Nevertheless, his penetration into the most fundamental questions arising from the profits and productivity of capital investment are immensely significant.

In addition to the fundamental argument presented by Wilken, there are a number of other equally compelling arguments for a universal share in profits. We can also make a case that the universal beneficiary deserves a share of profit because:

- The universal beneficiary is inevitably the recipient of the liabilities associated with the profit, i.e., pollution, climate change, and depletion of resources

- Production, and hence profit, exploits the limited resources of the natural world (on which the universal beneficiary has a related claim)

- The implementation of capital has a "market-crowding effect," which creates barriers to entry by others

- The conditions for a productive economy arise from a tremendously complex set of socially constructed circumstances, such as the education of the work force, infrastructure, and a culture that generally allows enterprise to function smoothly

In summary, we can see that profit arises in the context of the total system in which it operates. It is not solely the rightful property of labor (as Marx would have it), or of those who put up the money (as capitalists would have it), or of those who contributed original ideas and technology, or of "management." Nor are, it should be noted, the legitimate claims of society satisfied by government taxation. All these parties have a legitimate claim, but the argument here is that there is an additional valid claim, that of the universal beneficiary.

Natural Resources

Aside from profit and productivity per se, we can also assert that the universal beneficiary has a rightful claim on resource extraction generally and on penalties for degradation of the natural world.[2]

In keeping with what we now know about the interdependence of the natural realm, this case can be made convincingly concerning the provenance of all the resources of the physical world, including minerals, land, water, air, and so on.

Intellectual Property

Finally, since intellectual property always draws on the universal legacy of human knowledge, and cannot be fully separated from that legacy, we can also say that the universal beneficiary has a right to an incremental share of it. This partial claim is valid, even when "owned" through patent or other intellectual property rights. It is fine to assert that intellectual property is rightfully and primarily owned by its creator, but it is illogical to conclude that this ownership is absolute.

---

2): see Peter Barnes, *Who Owns the Sky?* Washington: Island Press, 2001.

The Pragmatic Conclusion

At this point, we should step back and consider exactly what is meant by these assertions of valid claims, and how this relates to the practical proposal for civil endowment. What is being asserted here is that in terms of absolute and pristine justice, the universal beneficiary has claims to some finite portion of profit, of natural resources, and of intellectual property. However, I have never said that it is practical to determine the extent of those claims. In fact, it is *highly impractical* to calculate such proportions, and it would be even less so to actually collect them. Therefore, what is practical is to create bodies of capital that are fully endowed to the universal beneficiary, as a way of satisfying these legitimate and intrinsic claims, but in ways that are fundamentally voluntary.

This creates a different, simpler route to a just outcome in practice. If, through compassion, we extend an equal intention to all human beings that they might have economic wellbeing, we could grant each individual a membership, as it were, in this universal beneficiary. It is perhaps axiomatic to my thinking as a Buddhist that the point of view based on justice and that based on compassion would converge, at least at the pragmatic level. We could acknowledge everyone's membership in this universal group—both because they rightfully deserve it (economic justice) and because out of kindness we want them to have it (compassion).

As well, once we accept that the universal beneficiary has a stake, the question of the size or proportion of that stake takes on an entirely different flavor: we could see that the stake is as large as our kindness! It is as large as our generosity to ourselves and to future generations. It is as large as is ethically responsible for it to be, in keeping with respect for private property and individual rights. And at some point in the future, perhaps we will make it as large as it needs to be to make the economy work the way it must.

Because the formation of civil capital represents a fresh start and an unbiased and positive inspiration for an interdependent economy going forward, it represents a tremendous healing potential for humanity. This type of capital honors the legitimate claims of the universal beneficiary, but it can be established without appropriation or disputation, by reason of compassion.

There is no need to wait for society as a whole to say, "Oh, yes, that's right, everyone deserves a piece of the economy, everyone deserves wellbeing." Instead, this is something that can be created on the basis of individual initiative, inspired leadership, and cooperative action. It can exist and flourish in our crazy, mixed-up world and have as great or as little effect as we collectively give it. It is an expression of freedom, not a restriction of freedom. In the exercise of that freedom, the aspiration for economic justice and its tangible manifestation can converge.

The Reasoning from Causality

In this segment, we explore the reasoning behind the idea that civil capital is a good idea from the point of view of causality. In other words, we ask how and why it could function in a causal way to create significant benefits to society.

When we talk about any sort of causal analysis in economics, we are entering complex territory. This is especially true the further we get into the macroeconomic side of things, which is really where civil endowment theory "lives." Therefore, in this section, we will enter into the subject gradually, and establish a foundation for the discussion. First, will look into causality in economics in a general way, and then consider causality in relation to capital. Finally, we will look at civil capital in that regard.

Economies as Systems

As we approach this topic, we could ask ourselves in a general way what we think an economy is. The answer that economists have given to this question—for a very long time in fact—is that economies are systems. It is only rather recently, though, that some economic thinkers have begun to regard the system in question as including the whole of the human race, functioning as part of the ecosystem of planet Earth. We could use the term "planetary economy" for this system, in part simply because the term "global economy" is overused to the point of numbness, but also because the term planetary economy suggests that the planet itself has something to do with it, which it certainly does. If the term itself does not invoke that meaning entirely, we should be explicit that it refers to the human economy of our world in all its aspects, a whole system that is integral with the physical environment of the planet and its ecosystem.

We should give early economic thinkers credit for their often brilliant work in trying to understand how economic systems function. They have been pioneers in reasoning in terms of systems, seeing interdependence, and so on. It is just that they weren't looking at the whole system. As well, they were looking, by and large, at the system in ways that reflect the intellectual roots of economics in 18th century scientific thinking. The results of this way of thinking led to the reduction of the function of an economy to the mechanistic operation of a set of quasi-independent entities with very simplified motivations (usually along the lines of pure self-interest). This is convenient in the sense that it makes it possible to reduce everything to mathematical models and equations. These are systems of course, but they are abstractions drawn from and then projected back onto the real economy. They do not reflect—or they reflect in incomplete ways—the role of the human mind in an economy and that of the Earth's ecosystem. The step forward in system thinking that at least some economic thinkers have taken since roughly 1950 is to include the role of human motivations in more complex ways than simple "rational maximizing," and to include the natural world as an integral part of any economic system valid enough to analyze.

We should not give mere passing mention to the role of the mind in economic systems. Just as we have pointed out the psychological dimension at the heart or essence of capital, we can expand our awareness of the role of the mind to all our economic actions. Feedback loops and tipping points, two key concepts in system theory, bear very strongly on human behavior in groups. Events like stock market crashes, bank runs, or—on the more positive side—spontaneous outpourings of generosity in times of disaster, all attest to this. In fact, the activity of the human mind is intrinsic to all our social and economic systems. It is not immutable, despite the fact that habits are very strong. Trends of thought change over time. Ideas (both good and bad) spread like wildfire. Economic conventions and institutions are, at their root, the result of our thinking.

Causality in Economic Systems

One way to begin describing the workings of causality in economics systems is to say that it is non-linear. By analogy, this means that it isn't like billiard balls hitting each other and moving off in simple, predictable ways. System causality is non-linear for a number of reasons. The first of these is that a whole system includes conditional factors which, broadly speaking, include the environment, which contains the processes under consideration.

(Here we are speaking in abstract terms, not necessarily in terms of the natural environment. For example, an environmental factor for a chess game would be the chess board, or the table it sits on.)

Another reason for this is that causal factors in a system have multiple, not singular, effects. Therefore, we need to talk about outcomes in terms of a field or matrix of effects. Those effects ripple out and reverberate as subsequent causes within the system itself. None of this is simple or linear.

The two main types of causal factors are causes and conditions. In particular, causal theories of both Eastern and Western origin talk about the important role of conditions. Here is an example often used in Buddhism: in the germination and growth of a plant, we can point to the seed as a primary cause, but that process will not take place without the enabling conditions of soil, water, sunlight, and so on.

Conditions are of major significance in economic thought as well. In fact, if you search for an explanation of why certain things happen in economics, at least some of the factors usually turn out to be conditions, not causes. The same is true for the search for ways to achieve desired outcomes. Often that involves fostering the proper conditional factors. This is what we usually see with economic policy and investment decisions: they are aimed at creating conditions for a particular outcome. That is certainly true, for example, in how the Federal Reserve makes calculations about how its decisions will affect financial market participants and, ostensibly, the broader economy. All this is far removed from some sort of "billiard-ball" view of causality, but it fits nicely with a view that sees conditionality as integral to the causal process. Understanding this point will help us see how civil endowment is meant to work.

To focus now on causes, let's briefly take a look at a metaphorical big-picture schema for how they operate in the economic process. I would like to identify three broad types of "ways of working" for causes, without making any assumption that this is a complete list. This is just a set of ways of thinking about how causality operates. The three types are: from the edge, encompassing, and from the center. To understand this, it would be helpful to conceptualize or visualize the economy as a sphere, with countless interconnected relationships and events, all in dynamic motion.

Causality that operates from the first two of these ways—from the edge of a system and by encompassing it—are acting more externally on that system than causes that come from the interior of the system, so we can call the first two types "exogenous" and the last type "endogenous."

Let's start with "edge" causality. The smaller and less coordinated actions are, the more we can say they operate from the edge. For example, the actions of individual economic actors take place at the edge. Although they affect the whole, such effects can usually only be seen when highly aggregated. For example, if one person changes his or her light bulbs from old-fashioned incandescent bulbs to LEDs, there is not much reduction in overall electric demand. If the majority of people did so, that would greatly change things. The general principle is that the smaller and more functionally independent actors are, the more we can say their causal inputs are "from the edge." Even the activity of very large players, such as a major investment fund, is to some degree from the edge as well.

One of the observations of classical and neoclassical economics that has real value and significance concerns the benefits of freedom of action at the edge. There are real economic efficiencies

CIVIL ENDOWMENT

that arise from this, efficiencies that are quite apart from, and in addition to, the very real importance of freedom at a human level. One of the features of Austrian Economics—which is related to (but not identical with) Neoclassical Economics in its views—is its approach of breaking everything down in a very granular way in terms of the motivations and actions of individual actors in the economy, and to place an ultimate level of importance on the freedom of those actors.

Although this view has some level of truth to it, it fails as a sufficient principle, simply because there is little attention paid to the overall system in which they operate, and because individual actors acting in their own interest tend to aggregate economic power and impair the freedom of others. And power, of course, has never been fairly distributed in the first place. As well, some theories make assumptions about perfect knowledge of the market and so on, which is absurd. In any case, it is important to recognize that

EDGE CAUSALITY: an agent acting from the exterior of a system.

early thinkers in economics had important insights about causality at the edge, even if we reject the broader conclusions of their intellectual descendants in Austrian and Neoclassical schools of the discipline.

As the scale of power and activity become larger in relation to a system, we come to the encompassing type of causality. A monopoly is a prime example of this, since the power of the monopoly to dictate price and suppress competition spans or encompasses the whole market by definition. Laws and regulations are also examples of encompassing causality, since they apply to situations across

ENCOMPASSING CAUSALITY: an agent grasping the whole system.

CIVIL ENDOWMENT

the board in whatever jurisdiction they operate. The extreme situation of encompassing causality is a command economy, such as a monarchy or dictatorship.

At this point it may become clear that the principle power relations in our contemporary economy function predominantly by way of these two types of exogenous causality. Private enterprises function mostly with edge causality, which in its extremes has the character of extraction and exploitation. At that point, it takes on a parasitic relationship with the broader economy. Then, to manage the excesses and perversions of private enterprise, we have laws and regulations (encompassing causality), which try, with only limited success, to keep the whole thing under control.

The notion of endogenous or centralized causal activity is a little harder to see. To give an example from outside economics, think about a seed inside a piece of fruit. Under certain conditions, that seed will germinate and expand its way outward through the fruit. That is a literal example from the physical world of a cause acting from the center. When we speak metaphorically about an economic system, it is not quite so obvious what the center is. It is easy to see what the edge of a system is in this set of metaphors—it is small, discrete actors and events. What we mean by the center here is something like "the essence of the process."

I would like to make a general assertion that endogenous, centralized causality is more powerful than the exogenous sort, but I must be honest that I don't have a well-developed formal argument to back it up. Perhaps the reason that this feels correct intuitively is that the center of a system has more direct bearing on the whole system. An example of this is in the game of chess, where actions at the center of the board are more significant than those at the edges.

CAUSALITY FROM THE CENTER:
an agent functions from within the heart of the system.

Another example is splitting a log of wood. It would take a tremendous amount of work to split the log starting from anywhere but the center. Another (but less ecologically correct) example is blowing up a rock formation. To do that, you drill into it and put the explosives inside. That is an endogenous cause.

It may help to see what is meant by "the center" here by considering how capital investment works. The well-known phrase "seed capital" is too apropos to pass over at this point. I would like to put forth the idea that capital is a central causal agent in the sense of this discussion. Activity and effects expand outward from its operation. From a causal point of view, the operation of capital operates at the center of the economic process for that particular investment. It determines the course of the production of goods and services for the life of the investment, and it does so at a qualitative level. It also determines the environmental and social effects that arise, both from the production process and those arising from the product itself.

Therefore, we can say that capital is an endogenous set of causes within an economic process. And, in aggregate, it is causally endogenous to the economy generally. In many ways, this explanation of the central causal role of capital is just a deepening of the first step in "The Leap," where we saw the primacy of capital in a modern economy.

One-to-all causality

Once we have some clarity about causal factors (causes and conditions), and broad categories of causal processes, we still need to think about how they all function at a whole-system level. Here, a breakthrough in thinking is possible, but only if we see something fundamental about systems. The truth that needs to be seen is this: in an interconnected system (which the economy is, and always has been), *every causal factor affects the whole.*

We need to consider this idea carefully. Typically, we think that actions or conditions definitely have effects, but those effects are seen as particular or localized. We tend to think they are "specialized" in some sense. For example, we may think that consumer confidence in the U.S. has some bearing on employment in China. We think in those kinds of terms, but not in terms of pervasive, system-defining outcomes.

It is true that we may not see all the effects of every action, or that small actions may have no observable effects. But effects, even when infinitesimal, are effects. Effects become causes of other effects, which then become causes in turn. We can use the term "ripple out" for this kind of field of effects. Causality in systems operates at the level of the whole system.

To give an example of one-to-all causality, the easiest to use (and the one perhaps most widely understood these days) is in the emission of carbon dioxide and other greenhouse gasses in the activity of the modern economy—especially the burning of fossil fuels. The carbon dioxide goes into the atmosphere and, by the activity of wind currents, becomes admixed in a homogenous way globally. The carbon dioxide from my car exhaust increases carbon dioxide levels infinitesimally but inexorably throughout the world. Carbon dioxide levels create the conditions for temperature rise through the greenhouse effect. Temperature rise then presents the conditions for other outcomes. As temperatures increase, the melting of permafrost will release vast amounts of methane, an even more potent greenhouse gas than carbon dioxide. These kinds of feedback loops and tipping points exist throughout systems. The fact that I drive a car that emits carbon dioxide makes me as fundamentally culpable in system change as everyone else.

We need to contemplate carefully this notion of whole-system impact of specific events and actions. We need to look at it from a neutral point of view, with honesty, and without hope or fear. If we see it, we can begin to see that just as specific events and actions can have a negative effect on the whole system, they can also have a positive effect, and not just in an incremental way, but in a transformative way. The very nature of a system can be transformed. It is not as if one thing over here affects one thing over there, and nothing else. One thing affects the whole thing. Once we see that, we can think seriously about the causal basis of positive system change.

Capital and Causality

We have explored the idea that capital plays a central role causally in modern economic systems. Let's go into more detail with that, exploring it again from the point of view of the three characteristics of capital—namely, its manifestation, nature, and essence.

The manifestation of capital, as we have discussed, is economic power. This power is not just the power to produce, but also the power to define what is produced and the circumstances of that production. Now, isn't power just another way of talking about causality? Power is the capability to make something happen. In the case of capital, this power is very broad based. It has a defining and ordering quality. And, of course, the profits arising from capital can create all kinds of power in society, for both good and evil. Primarily, though, when we refer to capital manifesting as power, it means the power to make the productive process happen, and to directly define that process.

Then we should consider the nature of capital, which is its social construction. Capital in any modern sense of the concept could not exist without a very complex web of social inventions, conventions, and institutions. Money itself is a prime example of this. Conventions and legal protections around property are another broad set of socially constructed conditions that enable capital to exist. The very workings of a commercial economy, of markets, of producers and consumers—all these are part of a social fabric.

The practice of putting forth money for investment depends on multiple and delicate layers of interpersonal trust, social networks (in the old-fashioned sense of that term) and laws and regulations. Note that these are mostly conditions that enable capital to function as a cause. That is interesting in terms of the foregoing discussion of causes and conditions, isn't it? Within a matrix of appropriate social conditions, capital operates and manifests its power.

> *When something is complete, it is a perfection of that thing's inherent potential.*

Finally, we get to the essence of capital, which is its psychological root in the four-fold geist. All these four dimensions operate causally in capital. The "pervasive intention" is perhaps the simplest. Productivity happens because people intend it to. The culturally transmitted "embedded knowledge base" comes together with the "operational plan," providing the general and specific knowledge to implement the productive process. Guiding the whole process is the "foundational spirit." This last dimension of the capital geist sets the tone in several key areas. These include: the social spirit of the enterprise, the time frame of investment calculations, the provenance of the allocated wealth, and the determination of the beneficiary. Seen within this essential psychological framework, capital is revealed as a highly specified and contextualized set of intentional implementations of economic causality. The complex character of those intentions is determinative of the results of that causal process. Needless to say, this does not mean that the results of a deployment of capital are exactly in line with the intentions or expectations involved. It simply means that this complex set of intentions creates whatever result *does* come about.

Causality and Civil Capital

At this point we can apply all these general arguments and ways of thinking to the civil-capital concept.

In a very real way, civil capital is an optimization or perfection of the causal dimension of capital. Using the concept of perfection may seem a little questionable or extreme here. Actually, I stand by that characterization, but it may be helpful to see that the meaning of "perfection" as used here tends toward the sense of "completion." When something is complete, it is a perfection of that thing's potential to be what it inherently is. An overarching theme of this book is that capital—both in its theory and its deployment in society—has been burdened by our incomplete understanding, and thus our imperfect implementation. We do not understand what it could be, so we have failed to facilitate its complete potential.

In particular, the presupposition that the foundational spirit of capital must have only one particular quality—namely, an extractive and self-serving one—collapses capital theory into a flatland, a monochrome of limited possibilities. The emergence of socially responsible investing, whatever its limitations, is proof in practice that investment with broader intentions than profit taking actually works. The foundational spirit of civil capital is a fundamental step beyond SRI, and I believe it arrives at the logical completion of that possibility.

When we talk about the completion of the capital idea here, there are actually two closely related meanings. The first is to see the full possible spectrum of the foundational spirit of capital, all the way up from utterly reptilian, extractive/exploitive thinking to the benevolent and fully expansive mentality of civil capital. The second meaning of "completion" is to see the particular nature and implications of civil capital itself. It is in this second meaning that the notion of "perfection" applies most directly.

We can describe the perfection of civil capital in three aspects: the perfections of provenance, beneficiary, and implementation.

The perfection of provenance means that the wealth that forms civil capital is to be given freely; it arises from generosity. It is not stolen or appropriated through force. As well, the profit arising from civil capital will accumulate through fundamentally positive forms of livelihood. All this is extremely important as to how civil endowment functions and is viewed by society going forward. There will certainly be imperfections in practice, dis-agreements about investments, and criticism. This fact simply underscores the importance of not cutting corners at a funda-mental level. The outcomes that civil endowments could create include qualities that are usually regarded as intangibles, such as trust in society, hope for the future, and trans-cultural good will. For all these reasons, pure provenance is an essential part of the causal matrix we must try to create.

The perfection of beneficiary means that the ownership and productive return of civil capital is fully dedicated to every human being, now and in the future. This particular feature will contribute to the system feedback loop of encouraging broad-based support. Certainly, the idea will require education and familiarization, but the argument here in terms of causality is that the very universality of the intended benefit will ensure that it is a meme that will spread widely.

Finally, there is the perfection of implementation. This refers to the design to be in service of the whole system, including society seen as a collective, and the whole of time, i.e., with the longest possible term thinking. The notion of Implementation here also includes the feature of civil society governance. We will discuss that topic in depth in the next chapter.

There is a distinction that needs to be drawn here between "every human being" and the consideration of society as a whole or collective. The term "collective," of course, harkens to "collectivism," which carries a good deal of historical baggage in economic discourse. To the extent I do use this term, I use it in its strictly literal sense, and in terms of a whole system, a system of which, as we've seen, human beings are only a part. It is extremely important at this point in history to see the inescapable interrelatedness that includes us all. There are tremendous synergies and efficiencies that come about from acting in accordance with that fact. This must be seen as a fact that is completely independent from the question of human unity in spirit or social organization.

As best I can envision it (and this may create some challenges in interpretation), I would like the foundational spirit of civil capital to address itself **both** to every human being individually, **and** to human society seen as one system. Not one or the other. The first principle has great significance for the implementation of justice and the exercise of compassion. The second, whole-system aspect has tremendous importance in a causal principle we will discuss below, namely, the efficiency of universal scope.

The argument from causality with regard to civil capital comes down to the point that it is designed in accordance with the very essence of the nature of economic causality. In particular, the principle that causal factors operate in a one-to-all, ripple out, manner implies that capital could be consciously designed to work with that principle. The possibility that we could design a type of capital to impact the whole in a positive way brings us to a very delicate, profound, and decisive point: the EFFICIENCY OF UNIVERSAL SCOPE.

What is meant by this? Although many of the efficiencies described as resulting from the six virtues in an earlier chapter are highly qualitative (such as "sufficiency" resulting from generosity), this type of efficiency has both quantitative and qualitative aspects. At its basic level, it also accords with the most commonplace kind of wisdom.

Say you just picked a hundred strawberries. Now, anyone with (as they say on the farm) "a lick of common sense" would know to put those strawberries in a container to take them home from the field. An alternative approach would be to carry them back one handful at a time. That would be less efficient. The universal scope in this case simply pertains to the function of the container. It contains all the strawberries.

Many of the purported benefits of say, socialism, have been argued on similar merits. But notice that power in that case is applied exogenously, through the state. In the case of civil endowment, the power is being applied endogenously—from within the very center of the economic process. The administration of endowments by civil society is not meant to regulate the economy through authority, but to influence the economy by making an ongoing series of direct investments, and to do so not from one centralized organization, but from any number or organizations sharing similar goals.

It is very intriguing to contemplate how civil capital can create and harvest vast efficiencies of universal scope. Such consideration leads me to an admittedly hypothetical idea—but one that is, even so, most compelling: the idea that civil capital *will, in the long run, pay for itself.* It could do so by way of compounding this efficiency of universal scope. Civil endowment investments could tap into efficiencies and productivities that have so much leverage that we will see that it is worth creating civil capital out of whole cloth – for example, through fiat-currency loans to civil endowment organizations.

In summary, we can say that the qualitative features of capital are its causal features. Capital is causality because capital, in its outer manifestation, is power. In its nature, the features of capital are the socially constructed conditions that enable productivity. Finally, in essence, capital is the application of the human mind to the challenge of livelihood. The civil capital idea is in a very real way an optimization of these general features of capital.

Making an argument that civil capital will benefit society because that is how it is designed may seem somewhat circular. That might be so if we were only viewing the matter superficially. It would also be so if the characteristics of capital were not what they are. But the essence of capital—its psychological DNA as it were—is the fundamental wellspring of its operation. Thus, discussing its causal efficacy in terms of its design and intent is very much to the point.

Conclusion

To sum up this chapter, we can draw some very straightforward conclusions from the three sets of reasoning in support of a civil endowment system. The reasoning from compassion is to convince and remind ourselves why this system ultimately should be created, but also why it is realistically possible to do so. The reasoning from justice is to convince ourselves that creating such a system is an ethically positive course of action. Finally, the reasoning from causality is to develop understanding and confidence about how such an idea can actually work in practice.

THE SPECIAL PROPOSAL

CHAPTER SEVEN

The Special Proposal

THIS CHAPTER HAS TWO PARTS. THE FIRST IS A DETAILED EXPLANA-tion of a civil endowment system in practical terms. It answers basic questions as to how we can implement the set of ideas discussed so far. Because this proposed system is something that does not yet exist, and which could be transformative in a very significant way for humanity's future, I consider it "special." The second, much shorter, part is the direct proposal that we go ahead and create such a system. The proposal is made in a short "exhortation" that directly states that we *can* do this, we *should* do this, and we should start *immediately*. These two parts—the detailed description and the exhortation—make up The Special Proposal.

The Civil Fiduciary

The practice of fiduciary relationship is quite ancient in Western society. It involves one party taking care of the interests of another party, and there is a whole tradition of ethical and legal bonds that establish and protect that relationship. The meaning of the term can be very broad, but it is most commonly used these days to refer to someone prudently taking responsibility for the wealth or money of another. The most prominent example of this is, of course, the financial services industry, which includes such functions as banking, brokerage, and wealth management.

The civil fiduciary function is a special case of this type of rela-tionship, in which the party whose interests are being served is the universal beneficiary. The idea of establishing such a fiduciary sets the tone for describing how the goal of investing for the uni-versal common good could be made practical. Doing so does not require society as a whole to have unity, cooperation, or organiza-tion around such an idea, merely that someone, or some group of people takes the responsibility for it.

The system I envision is one of organizations made up of teams of people who each individually understand and are committed to the civil endowment idea, and who work cooperatively to carry out the work of civil capital in all its aspects. The relationship between the motivation of individuals and the structure of the organiza-tions in which they work is especially important. Individuals and organizations can both go wrong, but if the organization is structured correctly, an organizational culture is established that is appropriate to its goals. If the individuals involved are commit-ted to participation and leadership with integrity, there is a chance for success. In fact, there are many hugely successful, productive organizations in the world today. A lot is known about the subject of their healthy functioning. Therefore I am optimistic about the possibility of creating successful civil fiduciary organizations.

What I refer to as the civil fiduciary generally is, then, the net-work of all such organizations. There should be any number of these in a growing, evolving movement spread around the world. I have repeatedly used the term decentralized to describe this network. This point is absolutely fundamental. Attempts to cre-ate top-down central planning have been proven to be structural failures. This includes socialism generally on the national scale, but also the sorts of international institutions we have today, such as the World Bank, the World Trade Organization, and the like. They do not serve the interests of humanity effectively because they operate within the mindset of the most powerful players in the economy—and usually serve the interest of those players.

The civil fiduciary should be decentralized simply because that is the most skillful way to organize it. In our discussion of causality, we explored the idea that all causal factors affect the whole system. The implication here is that all instances and aggregations of civil capital will impact the world situation. That is true whether they act under any central authority or not. The defects of central planning and command economies generally are well known at this point in history. Therefore, the assertion of this proposal is that the guiding principles of civil investment are sufficient to unify the system.

Toward the end of this chapter, we will discuss how loose form of governance might be instituted within the civil fiduciary, and how the integrity and reputation of civil endowment can be protected by various kinds of certification and oversight. For now, the main points to consider are that the system under discussion is one of multiple organizations (perhaps eventually hundreds or thousands of them), and that they all take the universal beneficiary as their object of fiduciary responsibility. They will aggregate wealth and form civil capital for that purpose.

The Types of Endowments

Given that the unifying principle of civil endowments is their responsibility to the universal beneficiary, and not to a central authority, we might then ask if all the endowments will be exactly the same, or if they will exist in various types and categories. I believe it makes most sense to have a great deal of diversity in the typology and structure of endowments. The most obvious reason for this is that, although the UB is the ultimate beneficial owner in all cases, endowments would have a wide range of types of assets under management. It would make sense for endowment organizations to have areas of expertise and focus, such as renewable energy, agriculture, and so on. Perhaps even more significant would be a typology based on the social focus of investment. Specifically, endowments could have a focus of investment that is worldwide, local, or individual. What this means is that an endowment could focus its outward investment process (1) on the whole world and human society, (2) on a particular region, or (3) on the needs of a particular person.

Because the beneficiary is the universal one, the most obvious—and indeed the first—endowments that should be created are ones that take the planetary economy as a whole as a focus. That being so, the nature of a capital investment is that it has to be localized in some sense of the word. If we take, for example, a wind farm owned by a civil endowment, it has to be *somewhere*. That is true even if it is intended to reduce greenhouse gas emissions for the whole planet, and even if the profit or productivity of that wind farm were to go to a revenue fund that could be shared with every human being on the planet. This is a somewhat simplified example, but gives a good idea of an investment with a global or universal focus.

The universal beneficiary will be the ultimate owner of all types of endowments.

Because there are different kinds of need—and especially levels of need—around the world, and because the customs and institutions in various places are so different, it also makes a great deal of sense to develop endowments that have a local focus of investment. This is in keeping, of course, with the decentralized spirit of the movement, and it is a highly practical way of doing development correctly. It is important for people in a particular region to contribute to an endowment for investment in their region, even as they gain understanding that the beneficial owner of the capital is the human whole. Because of the universal quality of civil capital, it would also be entirely appropriate for wealth to come into a particular local endowment from other endowments, especially from relatively richer parts of the world. Having contributors (and, effectively, stakeholders) in the endowment from outside the region could also contribute perspective, oversight, and reduce risk of corruption. But this would only be so if local people were also contributors and had direct involvement. This last point is another example of the co-centric principle at work. Healthy economic development is not going to come entirely from outside a region—we've seen the results of that. Nor can it come strictly from within a region, either from the point of view of basic wealth of resources, or that of technologies, skills, and ideas.

In this context, "local" simply means a geographical area less than the whole world. It could refer to anything from a town or village up to a whole continent or region of the world. There could be an endowment for Sub-Saharan Africa, for example, or for a small city in Russia. The formation of these endowments would arise from local leadership and initiative, but seed funding from other endowments or from foundations would play an important role.

The value of local endowments is that the circumstances and needs for creating specific investments would be clear. There are tangible questions that can be raised. What do the people of this region need to have sufficiency and opportunity? How can the region become a better global citizen in terms of environmental impacts? How can existing institutions be engaged? There are localist and regionalist movements already in action around the world. Local civil endowments could give those movements a lot more power and efficacy.

I do not envision that the emphasis would be on local endowments being formed in line with strictly political borders. As is well known, there already exist such funds based on political jurisdictions, in the form of sovereign wealth funds. These are very significantly different in structure and intent than civil endowments. Because the beneficiaries of these funds are limited to those living in that local area, and because most funds are invested in old-economy ways, they really aren't creating the kinds of benefits that are needed. Even more fundamentally, though, the division of the world into national economies is part of the problem. Let's get more creative! Bioregions make more sense. Small—even very small—regions make a lot of sense too.

I would especially caution against creating endowments based on ethnic or religious grounds, tempting as that may be. These divisions, again, are not in any need of reinforcement. There are ample ways of applying civil capital to the needs of disenfranchised minorities, for example, through community capital. We will consider community capital in more depth in the next chapter, but suffice to say here that it is one of the most attractive classes of assets that could come under civil endowment management.

The last main type of endowments to consider is the individual endowment. This is perhaps the type of endowment most prone to misunderstanding, but it is also potentially incredibly powerful. Therefore, the sequence I would advocate in developing this system would be to start with universal endowments, then local ones, and then the individual type.

With individual endowments, we really have to understand the idea of focus of investment very clearly. Such endowments would not be private property or trust funds in the conventional sense of that term. Nor would they be under the control of the individual.

Having said what they are not, let me try to describe what they are. An individual civil endowment would be a body of capital invested according to the principles of civil capital, in accordance with the needs of that particular person, at that person's stage of life. Here we can speak about the idea of global economic citizenship. How can the livelihood of that person be in accordance with good ecological practices? Even more basically, how will that person obtain sufficiency and opportunity? For example, what does a newborn child need? The answers are quite obvious: the child needs medical care, food, shelter, and a stable environment of human care. The reason that an individual endowment is powerful is that the demographic data (to use a rather impersonal term) associated with that person, at a particular time, gives very clear guidance as to how wealth could beneficially be invested. This data aggregates at local and regional levels and gives clear signals. It provides civil endowments with the information needed to help people skillfully.

As a person gets older, he or she needs educational opportunities, and then those for work. To have a livelihood—let alone one that is an exemplar of good global citizenship—there needs to be a level of investment necessary for that person to work and be productive. Throughout the arc of an individual's life, the specific circumstances of his or her personal and social context would be a very precise indicator and driver of needed investment decisions impacting him or her. For example, if an endowment organization managed, say, a million individual endowments, the data associated with those people would provide a rich source of ongoing guidance.

An individual endowment *per se* would never be private property, and at death it would roll over to be pooled and given to someone else. However, there are many specific and personal financial benefits that could come to a person indirectly from an individual endowment. It should be understood that all forms of civil endowments could potentially deliver a finite level of cash income to everyone on Earth. I say potentially, because initially the amount of this income would be extremely small and it would not be worth the transaction and administration costs of delivering the money or setting up accounts for everyone.

Civil endowments could potentially deliver cash income to everyone on Earth.

It is also questionable whether such a thing could even be accomplished at all in many parts of the world, for political reasons. However, it is important to see that this could in principle be done, given the information technology we now have. Assuming the amounts become large enough to make it worth doing, income from individual endowments could be moved into private trust funds for that individual, with various flexible possibilities for eventual direct disbursement.

There could also be ways for an individual to contribute to their own endowment. This would be an interesting motivator for bringing contributions into the overall system. People could also potentially invest in private savings vehicles that parallel the investment strategy of civil endowments. Finally, an individual endowment could also provide backing for various types of credit for that person.

Overall, the development of individual endowments would need to proceed in stages. Perhaps a first step would be for a regional endowment to designate assets or income to be placed into individual endowments. These could be awarded at birth, or on the basis of individual need, or universally across a given area of need. An interesting possibility would be to award individual endowments to people affected or displaced by natural disasters or conflict. This could be a very powerful step in empowering people to adjust, rebuild, or simply survive. Individual endowments could also be used to provide cash income to needy persons (or organizations that serve them) on a temporary, emergency basis, or to award cash pensions to the elderly (again, based on need).

Organizational Governance: The Fiduciary NGO

In this section, we will look into the questions of how a civil endowment could be structured organizationally, and how decisions about investments would be made. In a sense, the second question is the primary one in terms of the operation of an endowment. However, to get to that question we need to think about who would be making such decisions, how they would get into that position, and how they would work together. All these questions come down to the matter of organizational governance.

The most general point that has been made so far is that civil endowments will be controlled by non-profit organizations, or NGOs (non-governmental organizations). These types of organizations have different names and bases in law and custom around the world, which means that wherever they are chartered, they will have to abide by local law.

We will first look at some basic possibilities for governance style. These considerations apply both to how a person becomes part of leadership, and how individuals would interact organizationally.

Platonic Lineage Governance

The term "platonic lineage" is a hybrid of sorts, which in part reflects the cross cultural roots of civil endowment. The first part of the term is a cultural reference to Plato's *Republic*, which puts forth the general idea that leadership should be given to trained, experienced people who have the best interest of society at heart. This concept has been immensely influential in Western society. I use it here in a very loose way, and in no way do I bind myself to everything in the *Republic* which, after all, is an ancient text that reflects the thinking of its time.[1] The term "platonic" here is somewhat poetic, I suppose, and it conjures up a notion of a wise guardian—a steward or trustee. I invoke it here to refer to people who understand the principles of civil endowment and are motivated to be in its leadership. In practical terms, we can think in terms of how boards of directors of non-profit organizations are formed. Usually they are composed of people who are dedicated to a particular cause, and who are willing to work (most often without financial compensation) in service of an organization that pursues goals related to that cause.

There are various ways that people are chosen, but typically they have a strong interest to start with, and are nominated from within

---

1) In particular, I am aware that the *Republic* is considered the root of utopian literature in Western culture. I have been at some pains throughout to emphasize the non-utopian nature of the civil endowment idea. Nevertheless, it is a valid goal to try to describe some sort of ideal characteristics of a social process. In this case, those ideal characteristics are meant to relate very specifically to the administration of civil capital, not to society generally.

the organization in light of that interest. The leadership is self-selecting in this sense. It is not the people that select themselves, but more that the platonic leadership selects people according to its own criteria. As in the *Republic*, many forms of platonic leadership have an aspect of training. For example, consider the training of doctors. The medical profession is, broadly speaking, self-selecting, because you do not get to be a doctor unless you are educated—and ultimately accepted in your proficiency—by other doctors. The same is true for lawyers and many other professions. The university system is also platonic in that sense, especially at its higher levels. An individual only gets an advanced degree or a teaching post if, broadly speaking, his or her knowledge of the discipline in question is adequate in the eyes of those already in such a position.

The other part of the term, "lineage," may be correctly seen as a nod to the civilizations of the East, where the concept of lineage is very well established. This is especially so in spiritual traditions and associated disciplines such as martial arts—and in gentler arts like Japanese flower arranging. I have some hesitation about the term lineage because of my own reluctance to put the spotlight on myself as originator of the idea of civil endowment, and also because it may be seen strictly in association with Asian traditions.

The fact is, however, that in the way I am using it here, the notion of lineage pervades all cultural traditions. The kind of rigorous philosophical and practical training advocated in the *Republic*—and even in education generally—can be seen as a lineage transmission. There are lineages of all social and academic disciplines, of artistic disciplines and, more abstractly, of the process of technological invention. There are lineages of ideas and, of course, of spiritual inspiration.

Therefore, even if we to some extent associate "platonic" with Western civilization, and "lineage" with that of the East, we should see that there is a huge amount of overlap in the historically transmitted cultural practices that would pertain to something like civil endowment. There is the idea of knowledge and experience being sought after and accomplished in a particular person, and then that person passing it down in some way.

The key point of the platonic lineage model from a human point of view is that individuals will come to a position of leadership and responsibility through an orderly social process, one in which the skills of stewardship and trusteeship are developed and communicated, and are finally passed down in an authentic transmission. In this sense, the platonic lineage model is in line with all scientific, intellectual, and artistic traditions. Everyone in those fields has mentors, inspirations, and points of departure.For example, civil endowment theory itself has a lineage of ideas. The contributions of E. F. Schumacher, Hazel Henderson, Herman Daly, Folkert Wilken, Peter Barnes, and Elinor Ostrom figure very strongly in that lineage, to name a few important influences. Even though the civil endowment idea embodies original thinking of my own in a very fundamental way, it is still within the lineage of ideas of these and many other thinkers.

Aside from the knowledge and skills associated with leadership and stewardship, there is also the key element of motivation. Here, we may make an analogy with medical traditions, in which there is the transmission of a great deal of theoretical and practical information, but also the forming of commitments of attitude. In Western society there is the Hippocratic Oath. In the Tibetan medical tradition, it is axiomatic that a doctor would take the Bodhisattva Vow—essentially a commitment to benefit all beings—and act accordingly.

It is an interesting question as to how social innovation can happen with platonic lineage governance, in the sense that many of the examples given could lead one to feel that this is an inherently conservative approach to leadership. What about the rebels, the rabble rousers, and the non-conformists? Certainly in today's world, those who see the insanity of the current economic order might find themselves cast in such a light. They might even have personality traits of that nature, such as a resistance to orderly organizational behavior. A way to reconcile this possible contradiction is to see things in terms of the qualities that are needed in a leader for civil endowment.

What about the rebels, the rabble rousers, and the non-conformists?

Such a person would have to have creativity, analytic abilities, and social skills in working with others, along with a dedication to working for the common good of humanity.

My guess is that, given the possibility of working for such a cause as civil endowments, a lot of different types of people will come forward, and it will be an interesting mix. It may be the case that some well-intentioned people will not have the social skills to function as part of a team. In other cases, a person with good social skills may not have the needed level of understanding of economic issues to do the job well. In any case, the cause of civil endowment is fundamentally a compassionate one, and if people are in touch with that, they will have a chance to learn to work together, whatever their starting point or personality type may be.

With all that said, and since civil endowment is all about innovation and economic reform, the only element that could be called conservative in its governance would be the need to preserve the integrity of the idea, and indeed to evolve it through the cooperation of well-trained, properly motivated people working together and learning from experience. Humanity deserves as much, and we need to rise up in our higher potential to meet that need.

Democratic Governance

I strongly believe that, at least at the beginning, a platonic lineage system is the way to build out the institutions of civil endowment. However, as the system takes root even tentatively, it would be desirable to add in elements of democracy. Axiomatic to the ideals of both democracy and the civil endowment philosophy is the idea that people are inherently peers. We have an equal level of intrinsic worthiness and capability. Indeed, we should all have equal fundamental value and opportunity in any economic system worth working for.

In the administration of civil endowments, some aspects of democratic governance principles can be established fairly quickly. If (as they should) people who have entered into leadership through a platonic process treat one another as peers, they can then operate democratically, as do leadership councils of most civil society organizations. Down the road, systems could be set up wherein ordinary citizens become educated in the principles of a healthy economy generally and of civil investment specifically, and are able to become participants in some sort of process of economic democracy. Their education in matters of civil investment is analogous to the education of voters in democracy—a point, however, that does not exactly cause me to give rise to unbridled enthusiasm and confidence.

The question of economic democracy as a general possibility is well beyond the scope of this book. What is under discussion here is merely the idea of whether or not civil endowments could be administered democratically. My strong sense on this question is that this will not be generally feasible at the beginning. The civil endowment idea is a workable proposal to move us toward an economy that works for everyone, precisely because it does not naively assume that long-term policy decisions on investment can be made by just anyone, or through some sort of popularity contest. However, as support for the movement becomes widespread, there may be interest in creating endowments with democratic governance. This might be a worthy and interesting experiment at the proper time.

In the meantime, there are many attributes of a democratic or open-society framework that would be important to maintain, such as organizational transparency, open dialogue about investment theory and practice, and careful analysis of public feedback and input.

Commons-style Governance

As I searched for a subtitle for this book, one thought that came to mind was *The Capital Commons*. I hope learning of that piece of my creative process will convey my deep regard for the importance and potential of the commons tradition in relation to civil endowment. However, my continued research on the topic convinced me not to use that terminology in description of civil endowment, and the reasons for that can perhaps lead us into the rich world of commons thinking.

The commons has had a long and interesting history in human culture, and it is moving forward and evolving in striking new ways. Of course, many indigenous societies treat land and the natural environment as a commons (or something closely akin to it) as a matter of course. In European society, attitudes and practices around private property have been closely tied to the power and dominion of the aristocracy, a situation that in many ways is little changed in our present era. There have been, however, longstanding efforts to challenge the abuses of privilege and exclusion, such as the *Charter of the Forest*, enacted in England in the year 1217, which was a companion document to the more famous *Magna Carta*. It guaranteed certain common rights of access and use to ordinary people. (It is interesting to note that, in England, people who are not among the aristocracy are still called "commoners.") Many of those rights were in effect for centuries. Then, during the Industrial Revolution, countless commoners were pushed from the land in England when members of the aristocracy started to view themselves as landowners and decided they could make more money grazing sheep on the land than letting people use it. That was called enclosure, and it is a continuing pattern to this day. Today, we see enclosure in areas like the patenting of genetic information, GMO crops, and many others.

One reason we have difficulty understanding the whole topic of the commons (at least in our public discourse) is that we tend to think only in terms of private property versus some sort of government control. There is typically no consideration of a third option. But in fact, commons-style governance is an important aspect of the "third way" that I have long advocated, namely, an economy guided by civil society.

Economist Elinor Ostrom, who in 2009 became the first woman to win the Nobel Prize in Economics, dedicated the majority of her life's work to studying the commons. In particular, she observed local commons systems firsthand all around the world, and saw many parallels as to how they are governed. Toward the end of this chapter we will look at the eight basic principles she drew from her studies of subjects such as irrigation rights and fisheries in traditional societies, and how those might apply to civil endowments.

What really comes into focus in the study of this subject is that a given resource is not a commons until we recognize it and create agreements that allow it to function in that way. In other words, a commons is a social construct; it is not something that naturally exists as such. Nor can it be made so through some sort of unilateral declaration. Therefore, it would be presumptuous for me to designate this nascent idea of civil capital as a commons.

Commons-style governance could help create a civil-guided economy.

With all that said, it is very exciting to believe that the commons movement will continue to grow in coming years and benefit society in many ways. Such progress could very likely pave the way for the future for civil endowment governance.

Decision Making

Next, we will take a look at the fundamental underlying criteria for decision making regarding civil capital investments.

We have examined the causal process in investment generally and seen that in the operation of capital as a causal factor, there are three main categories of effects. There is what is produced— namely, the goods and services associated with that investment. There are also ripple-out effects on the environment and society. Finally, there is what can be called "trickle-back," namely, financial effects (profit or loss).

You will probably note that this way of thinking parallels the triple bottom line logic that is common in New Economy thinking these days. Ripple out covers people and planet, and trickle back covers profit. I personally prefer to use the idea of productivity as the third "P" in the triple bottom line, so this is a slightly different way of categorizing things. Trickle back can actually be regarded as a subset of productivity, or as a broadening of that category. We will take up this last point in more detail in the next chapter, "The Transformation," because it points to some very powerful possibilities for civil capital.

This set of types of effect (productivity, ripple out, and trickle back) forms the backdrop against which the values and goals associated with civil investment can be considered. It constitutes the scope of consideration, one that transcends the conventional emphasis on profit alone.

Outcomes of investment include: productivity, "ripple out," and "trickle back."

Next, we need to consider the actual drivers of investment decisions. In other words, the above types of effects are all to be considered. But, what leads us to pick out a specific investment to bring about effects in those areas? The three main drivers are: 1) universal sufficiency and opportunity; 2) economic justice; and 3) environmental benefit.

It should be mentioned from the start that these drivers are not presented in any order of priority. The nature of the design of the civil endowment system is such that specific investments would be sought out that provide benefit in all three areas. At the same time, there could be differing areas of emphasis. Keep in mind that this system is conceived of as a decentralized one. Although civil capital will be defined as serving these goals, it is not as if anyone will be dictating priorities among them.

Concerning environmental goals, it could be argued that climate change presents such an existential challenge to civilization that any investment portfolio for the UB should be heavily weighted toward mitigation of greenhouse gas emissions through funding renewable energy projects. That is a very compelling argument.

Then again, what about extreme poverty—the people who are starving today? I am trying to develop this system such that teams of people can follow their own wisdom on such choices, and that their choices will synergize with others who build endowments. For example, large renewable energy projects in the developing world—despite logistical and perhaps political obstacles—would be huge drivers of poverty reduction. India is one place that comes to mind in this regard.

When we think about climate risk, we also have to include agriculture and land use generally, which are huge contributors to greenhouse gas emission. Reforms and new practices in these areas could also have large impacts in the areas of economic justice and poverty reduction.

A major aspect of economic justice is, of course, wealth inequality. We will discuss this in depth in the next chapter, but here we should consider the idea that lessening the huge gaps we see today cannot really be considered or achieved in absence of the other goals.

Out of these goals, each endowment would set its own protocols for investment. The idea would be to make investments that have impact in all the major areas we have discussed.

There is one more criterion that is quite important, and that is non-frivolity. Economic frivolity is hard to talk about, but you know it when you see it, as the saying goes. There is something palpably obscene about the kinds of indulgences that go on in the world today given the context of rampant poverty, injustice, and environmental decline. If we consider the "needs" that are manufactured in the mind of people by advertising, it becomes clear that the frivolous economy is quite extensive.

That said, frivolity is still a tough concept to universalize or impose on others. I don't want anyone to tell me I own too many books on economics or, for that matter, that the single malt scotch I buy once in a while is too expensive. These kinds of personal choices are perfect examples of the validity of the private economy. A civil-guided economy, as I envision it, would never exclude or try to eliminate the private economy. At the far edge of the economy, it is important to allow individuals their economic freedom. However, it is entirely valid to stipulate that the productive output of civil capital would be non-frivolous.

As we have discussed, civil capital operates very much in relation to the scope of the whole economy, and at the center of the causal process. Because of that, frivolous production would contradict the fundamental design principles of civil capital. It is not my purpose here to come up with some sort of list of what is and is not frivolous production in relation to civil capital. But it is important for endowments to include that consideration in their protocols.

Organizational Processes for Decision Making

Once we get a general sense of the considerations involved with civil endowment investments, we could lay out proposed ideas for decision making that are somewhat technical and procedural. Perhaps such ideas would be good ones, but first we need to step back and consider exactly what is being asked at the human level of those who make these decisions. Decision makers are being asked to allocate resources to specific economic processes that are intended to have the effect of benefiting all of humanity on an unbounded time horizon.

At one level, that might seem like an impossible task. It may in fact be an impossible thing to do perfectly. However, we need to keep in mind that any and all investment decisions ultimately have the same scope of effect—they impact all humanity on an unbounded time horizon. It is just that conventional investors take the simple way out and only consider more constrained considerations of outcome. Typically, they look at financial returns for their client or themselves over limited time frames. Even at this level of investment philosophy, it is quite a challenge. The analysis, financial modeling, risk assessment, and regulatory compliance involved all require high levels of knowledge and sophistication.

If we now jump up to triple-bottom-line (3BL) investing, there are whole other layers of social and environmental considerations. This might again lead back to the thought that civil endowment investing is more or less impossible. There is no denying it presents a challenge to rise to another level of sophistication. But upon deeper contemplation, some clarification and even simplification start to emerge.

We could make a comparison with traditional investing, which is more or less an attempt to extract money from a system. It is done in competition with countless others who are trying to do the same thing, and without trying to nurture the system itself or caring about its long-term future. Clients want high returns and if they don't get them, they'll go elsewhere. Compared to that, doing the right thing in a big way might start to seem like smooth sailing. And with 3BL investing, there are always those pesky clients who want their secure, yearly percentage (that is often just as high as conventional clients expect), and of course, they want to be able withdraw their equity whenever they want.

In light of all that, the universal beneficiary starts to look like a pretty good client! She is infinitely patient, never wants her equity back, and really just wants us to do the right thing. She is willing to let us learn from mistakes. From that point of view, the human process of civil endowment investing might begin to seem more workable, without minimizing the challenges involved. Think about it this way: this is something we (the human race) have to learn how to do—because we have to do it. Because it is something that has to be done, we have to start trying. That is the proper attitude to take.

All the basic processes that are involved with conventional and 3BL investing will need to be part of the work and will need to be done well: the analysis, the risk assessment, and the social and environmental calculations. But they will be done in a whole different context. An unlimited time frame is a very interesting thing, as is the structural injunction to serve the UB and minimize or eliminate extraction, exploitation, and externalization. This whole level of analysis will take a lot of good work by very good human minds. It will take experience and learning from mistakes and successes. It will take a lot of trust and respect and listening.

Practically speaking, then, it is likely that there would be a particular job function within an endowment organization to seek out and bring possibilities forward, and those possibilities would then go through various stages of evaluation and screening, with a final decision being made by a senior council. Some endowment organizations may encourage creativity and individual talent by empowering individuals to make choices more unilaterally, subject to monitoring and accountability.

It may be that information as to investment prospects could be shared among different civil endowments, much as there are research firms that work for the conventional investor community. It is possible in this regard that much of the research currently being done by socially responsible and impact investing firms would be of great value to civil endowments.

However decisions are structured, there are several principles that will be important to ensure the integrity of the process. The first is transparency. This means that information about the investment must be as complete and accurate as possible, and that such information be made available to all appropriate parties. This does not necessarily mean that the entire process of investment would be public knowledge. Each endowment would need to develop guidelines for appropriate levels and kinds of transparency, all of which would have to be in keeping with legal regulations.

However the approval process is structured, appropriate levels of monitoring throughout would keep the process on track and provide points of information for transparency and accountability. Accountability is another whole basic principle, one with implications not only internally to an endowment, but to civil society generally.

Finally, there is the learning cycle. This whole endeavor is something of a leap of faith. It could also be called a leap of reason, which is why I have tried to provide supporting arguments from the various points of view. In any case, once the process begins, we have to realize that it is an exercise in learning. We simply cannot get this right without trying it. I am looking forward to all this with a great deal of excitement, if you must know. I don't feel that we are quite there to even make initial investments, but we could get there fairly easily. The very structure of civil capital is such that it will be beneficial to humanity, even if implemented imperfectly. But doing it well—and doing it increasingly well over time, on an increasingly larger scale—is the great hope of civil endowment. That is why we must begin. We should start the civil endowment investment process in order to learn how to do it.

The Provenance of Civil Capital

In many public places throughout the world, there are fountains where people toss coins. I often wonder what people think about when they toss a coin. Perhaps they make a wish, or just do it for good luck. It is interesting to me that a small act of giving is traditionally regarded as bringing good luck. But how does it do that? And to whom are people giving the coin? Another part of me wonders what actually happens to the coins over time. Does a custodian come along every year or so and gather the coins up? Do people steal them at night? Then again, to whom do the coins rightfully belong? This leads to other questions.

Would you give a penny to save humanity from catastrophic climate change? Would you give a penny to end extreme poverty? I'm asking these admittedly rhetorical questions to stimulate thinking about the gift-economy source of the wealth that will make up civil endowments. Is it really a good idea to create these endowments? Will they help humanity? The interesting thing about these questions is that if the answer to any of them in your mind is "yes," then a basic opening at the level of mind has occurred. This is why we begin the discussion of the provenance of civil capital with the symbolic gift, the gift that is easy to make—and to put it most precisely, the gift that is emblematic of

Would you give a penny to save humanity from catastrophic climate change?

one's engagement with this very idea. In that engagement, there is a transformation, a shift in perspective.

One thing that could emerge from that shift is a sense that any form of generosity makes the world a better place. But to specifically give something, anything, to all humanity in perpetuity is quite something. The benefit of the symbolic gift, the micro-donation if you will, is that it opens our eyes to all of that.

This is very important, because we humans, along with being very kind much of the time, are very smart. We think, "Well, will this idea, this system, ever get big enough to really make a difference?" We speculate about that, and if we believe it, we may give. My answer to that last question, by the way, is, "I don't know." I really don't. But what I do know—based on all the reasoning that has been presented—is that we need to try out this idea. It has merit. It has heart. If something is needed, then there is a reason to make it happen. An important part of the idea, the part that makes it all come into focus, is the idea that it can be based on generosity.

The primary reason it should be based on generosity is that the generosity itself is transformative. Just as it transforms an attitude in an individual at the level of a tiny, symbolic gift, that transformation is additive and synergistic as it expands within society. We humans really do have what it takes to build a sufficient, cooperative, sustainable global economy. As the generosity accumulates and becomes built into the system, not only will the tangible investments we have talked about have their effects, but also will the palpable sense of participation in a peaceful, prosperous economy become widespread.

Generosity comes from a pure intention, whereas other sources, such as taxation, are coercive. Later, we will explore the idea that civil capital can grow out of its own productivity, but that depends on the whole system being first set in motion. For all these reasons, giving is the valid, essential seed of civil capital.

Building on the practice of giving tiny, symbolic gifts, the transformative and educational aspect of generosity can also be stimulated by more traditional and larger-scale types of non-profit fundraising. Such work will also serve to spread awareness of the civil endowment meme, and it will be needed to achieve a level of scale such that endowments could actually be launched. Traditional vehicles such as grants, bequests, and donations from wealthy individuals would be ways for a particular endowment to progress toward an adequate size that the work could begin. It is not my purpose here to envision such methods in detail, partly because it is a genre of work with a lot of established practices, but also because I don't see it as the methodology that will really build out the system at the level of scale and diversity that is needed. For that, we need structuralized inputs.

Let's think about how that would work. Countless transactions take place in a modern monetary economy. The basic idea of structuralized generosity is to build in small contributions to civil capital into some of those transactions. Many businesses already give small fractions of profit or specific revenue streams to worthy causes. It has also been long advocated that very small fees be put on transactions in the financial sector and used for beneficial purposes.

One such proposal came from Nobel Laureate James Tobin, who proposed a tax around 0.5 percent on international currency trading with the intention of reducing short-term speculation and the volatility that such speculation fosters. Most of the arguments for and against such a tax have centered on whether or not it would reduce volatility in such financial markets, and not so much on what would be done with the money.

It has been estimated that such a tax could generate between 100 and 300 billion dollars per year. To give a relevant number in terms of scale, the United Nations has estimated that the cost of totally eliminating severe poverty worldwide would be about 225 billion dollars per year. All this is just to give some perspective on micro-transaction loads and their potential. Structuralized inputs to civil capital would not be taxes. Instead, they would be voluntary, and as such they would have to be instituted in different ways. The most direct way to do that would be to convince firms that have a policy of "giving back" to make civil endowments a recipient. As firms arise that are funded by civil capital, such arrangements would become more and more standard. In time, micro loads on all manner of financial transactions could become a stable and accepted foundation of the civil endowment system.

There is a strong justification of this by right, from the point of view of the universal beneficiary. As we discussed in the chapter on reasoning from justice, the nature of profit arising from any and all capital investment is such that a claim for the UB cannot be excluded. It could be argued that this "public purpose" is satisfied by taxation, but such an argument falls apart entirely when we look at the matter from a global perspective. Taxation is always local from a global point of view. As well, taxation is always in an ambiguous position as to whether it is a reciprocal transaction (payment for public services) or money extracted by force—and thus an instance of theft or coercion. Without questioning the validity of localized public interest, there is a strong case to be made for a global public purpose. This is absolutely unarguable when it comes to issues like climate change. If we also keep in mind the spirit behind civil endowment, the global public interest also includes questions of poverty and sufficiency, environmental justice, wealth inequality, and the economic quality of life of ordinary people everywhere. There *is* a universal public purpose, and it is not served by any existing government. (Nor, by the way, do I advocate a world government.) Therefore, there is a strong case for some finite fraction of profit being allocated to the common good. I argue that the most effective way to do that is not to set up systems for cash distribution or to give it to governments, but to endow it permanently as civil capital.

A similar point can be made regarding the extraction of natural resources. The way income from these processes is currently distributed is extremely varied, ranging from absolute private ownership of mineral rights on privately owned land (or minimal license fees on public land), all the way up to total nationalization in many countries. In the case of revenues collected from a particular region, the handling of it is also very diverse. Norway, for example, has a permanent sovereign wealth fund that comes from oil and gas revenues and is invested in global financial markets. Its value is now at more than $200,000 for each and every Norwegian citizen, and income from its investments is mainly dedicated to social programs such as health care, education, and pensions for those citizens.

> *There* is *a universal public purpose, and it is not served by any existing government.*

The State of Alaska also has a permanent fund, which provides an annual cash royalty to residents of the state. North Dakota does too. Less well known is the fact that many public school systems, especially in the Western United States, derive substantial income from mineral extraction. While many countries take strong control of mineral wealth and use it for public purposes, in some other countries it is treated more as the personal wealth of the rulers, ruling families, and their cronies.

Despite the complexity and entrenchment of the current situation, I believe there is a very strong case to be made for a universal royalty on resource extraction. Setting aside for the moment the difficulty of instituting such a royalty, I argue that once the idea of civil endowment becomes somewhat well known, the idea of collecting resource extraction royalties for the purpose of such endowments could greatly enhance the acceptance of the royalties themselves. This is especially true because the idea of permanent or sovereign wealth funds is fairly well established. We need to start asking why everyone worldwide doesn't deserve to share in the benefits of such funds.

I think many fair-minded people would agree that humanity as a whole should share in some way in resource extraction. Obviously the people and organizations doing the work of extraction need to be paid, local governments have a claim, and so on. But there is a universal claim by right, however small it may be, and even more certainly, there is such a claim arising from compassion.

Of course, we should keep in mind that this topic is complicated by the question of whether resources should be extracted at all. Some resources should definitely stay in the ground, in my view. But still, we need to take a pragmatic stance on the question. Realistically speaking, resources are going to be extracted, some with greater harm to the environment than others. I take the attitude that no one is really in control of what gets done in the most general sense. The legitimate universal claim on resource extraction is made more potent, not less, by the fact that there are liabilities associated with that extraction, liabilities that are spread around much more universally than the direct income arising from the resources. In other words, the UB is going to get the risk and liabilities no matter what, so at least as long as the extraction goes on, there should be compensation to the UB.

The legitimacy of a universal claim is far more important than the size of it. I honestly don't know what the size of the valid claim of the universal beneficiary might be, or if there even *is* such a magnitude. In practice, there will always be a negotiated outcome. Right now, we are at zero.

The way forward is to advance the argument in principle for a universal share of resource revenue, and then find ways to bring in voluntary compliance. Ironically, this might be more possible initially in areas where mineral rights are most absolute, such as in the United States. If specific extraction operations could be convinced to contribute a very small universal royalty, that would be a start. One area to start might be forestry, because there are many examples of such operations that are trying to be responsible global citizens.

Considerations like this might, of course, bring up the idea of civil endowments themselves investing in resource extraction. In the area of renewable resources, that is a definite possibility. In the realm of non-renewables, that is more questionable—although, who am I to say? Of course, ownership stakes might be valid in extractive industries for the purpose of shareholder activism.

Finally, we should consider structuralized inputs from intellectual property. If all intellectual property is built on the foundation of our common human intellectual heritage, isn't it true that a universal royalty would be justified? Again, there are tremendous cultural barriers to instituting this sort of thing by law, but great progress could be made with voluntary contributions. If successful writers, musicians, and patent holders could be convinced to give a small slice of their monetized returns to civil endowments, it would build cultural support even as it grew the endowments.

All these inputs are justified by the principles of compassion and inter-manifestation, but also more pragmatically by the contribution of stability that comes from a peaceful civil society. The very reasoning and arguments that these structuralized income streams are valid inputs to civil endowments are the same arguments that can be used to convince people to voluntarily institute them.

One very practical idea about structuralized inputs is this: although endowments could certainly do their own fundraising generally, and could try to make agreements for steady streams of income from these kinds of sources, it may turn out that specialized civil endowment foundations would be the right way to organize inputs. They could then pass the money on to endowments for investment. There could be specialized foundations in various areas, including natural resource royalties, corporate profit sharing, intellectual property, bequests of land and real estate, and so on. Their expertise could lessen one of the most difficult challenges endowments would face—namely, raising money—and let them get on with the challenge of the investment process itself. The existence of such foundations would also provide a level of oversight for endowments.

The Productivity of Civil Capital

In a conventional understanding of capital, investments are meant to grow in value over time. Unfortunately, such growth almost always involves some combination of exploitation, extraction, and externalization, as well as simple speculative increases in the prices of assets. In that light, any sort ethically defensible internal productivity deserves to be carefully questioned, at least in the way our economy is currently structured. Can civil capital be profitable without doing all that bad stuff? My answer to this is a provisional yes, at least in the long to very-long view. I believe that civil capital will discover and build on certain efficiencies of universal scope, efficiencies which, in the best case, could create productivities sufficient to produce huge long-term returns on investment—and they could do so without the kinds of abuses that convention capital takes for granted.

In the shorter term, the surprising answer is that it doesn't matter. Inputs will be coming in continuously, and the desired outcomes are qualitative, not an accounting of ever-increasing financial value. Civil capital is proposed as a practical innovation—

Civil capital will discover and build on certain efficiencies of universal scope.

a reformed capital process. Therefore, overall profitability is certainly not the primary goal. To the extent profitability might be seen as a way to increase the size of endowments, the tradeoffs involved with doing so would have to be examined very carefully.

There is one related point that bears mentioning: if civil endowments develop a good track record, and their investments become established in a verifiable way as valid and secure, there is no reason that endowments could not borrow money for that purpose. That indeed is how most capital formation is accomplished. This needs to be seen, however, as a long term prospect—but a good one nonetheless. There are many ways this could be accomplished, including the establishment of civil endowment-owned investment banks, which could then issue bonds or simple loans to finance worthy projects.

When we think about the provenance of civil capital, it all comes back to generosity. Even this last point about loans to endowments comes back to that. Is the universal beneficiary a good credit risk? Might someone give them (us) the benefit of the doubt? There are many forms of generosity besides just handing over something.

As we contemplate the scope and importance of the impact a civil endowment system could have, we might recollect the classic example of a towering oak coming from a single acorn. The acorn is the simple, focused attitude of generosity toward the universal beneficiary, arising in one person's mind.

The Arc of Civil Capital

Since the economic process is dynamic and historical, it would be helpful to think about how the investments of civil endowments might be handled over time. The first important point to keep in mind is this: although the time frame under consideration is unbounded, the furthest we can imagine, this does not mean that specific investments should—or could possibly—be made and simply left in place for the indefinite future. That is not at all the meaning of investing on an indefinite time horizon.

What is meant is that the intention of the whole portfolio of investments would be set up in that way. Specific investments would come and go. To give an example that only applies in a very limited way, a day trader on the stock market has more concern for the overall value of his portfolio than for the individual stocks he buys and sells. The assets of a civil endowment portfolio are, by contrast, of great concern to an endowment, but for various important reasons, divestment will still be a significant part of the process. Gaining a sense of the whole life cycle of investment and divestment will be one important part of building a portfolio theory for civil capital.

In developing a portfolio theory (which in many regards will be unique to each endowment), the composition of the full range of investments will be considered, as will the performance of these investments over time. By performance here, we mean the full range of effects emanating from each investment, and how it harmonizes with other civil investments and with the broader economy.

Divestment could come about for any number of reasons, which we will examine in detail later. But the preliminary point to be made here is that there will need to be a continuous process of improvement in investment protocols and in portfolio theory itself. With that said, I would anticipate that a civil endowment would be far more patient—and more concerned with human consequences—than any sort of conventional investor. As we will see, various kinds of divestment will actually be among the most potent tools of an endowment in working for the greater good.

The first form of divestment to be mentioned is in the realm of organizational generosity. If the civil endowment system is to grow, synergize, and impact the global economy, new endowments will need to be formed continuously for a long time. It would be a potent expression of the mission and spirit of the whole endeavor for an endowment to regularly spin off segments of its wealth to new or emerging endowments. This could be particularly effective when assets moved from wealthier parts of the world to poorer parts. A rather small percentage of a large endowment in a rich country could form a very significant endowment in a developing economy. It would not always be the case that investments would have to be liquidated to do this, but it would often be so, if direct investment were to be redirected to another part of the world.

Another avenue of "benevolent divestment" could be the transfer of an asset to a more static state of affairs, such as the sale of land to a responsible trust or conservancy. Civil endowments will undoubtedly be active in land and real estate investment, and in some cases it may well be decided that the best use of such assets is that they are permanently taken off the market. Endowments might even engage in real estate procurement to temporarily save land from destructive development, with the goal to find a final owner that will not regard it as a saleable asset at all.

The transfer of equity to private individuals is yet another area of divestment that will accord with the goals of civil endowments. A primary way this could be done would be by allowing employees of companies funded by civil capital to develop an equity stake. Lessening the wealth gap by creating innovative ways to offer the opportunity of an "equity wage" would be a very exciting possibility in this arena. Of course, company founders and entrepreneurs routinely get rich by leveraging the invested capital in successful companies. How can employee equity be structured in a more egalitarian way? This leads us into the whole topic of civil entrepreneurship.

Although civil endowments will likely own assets from among the full range of investment vehicles, including stocks, bonds, and financial instruments of all kinds, I believe there should be something of an emphasis on direct investment in new or existing productive enterprises, simply because that is, well, more direct. Not only does direct investment go straight to the qualities of production involved, it also gains influence on the organizational culture of the enterprise in question. In addition to working conditions, safety, and general employment policies, this includes matters of compensation, including equity compensation.

Civil entrepreneurs, who undertake the process of creating companies with civil capital, will be working with whole new perspectives toward the social dimension of the enterprise. The compensation policies will be much more egalitarian, and transition to employee-owned status would be an integral part of the normal course of events. Civil capital will have a temporary role to play in creating such companies, after which the underlying capital can be freed up for other uses.

This is a good example of how the very long term intentions of civil capital can be expressed by a shorter term involvement with a particular investment. Typically, an endowment would fund the company, and the employees would buy it back over time. This, of course, would depend on the success of the venture, and the tenure of the civil capital could be quite long in some cases. It could turn out that some sort of mixed ownership could prove to be the best outcome. If employees are adept at guiding the affairs of the company, they may take a majority stake and the endowment could share in profits from a minority stake. If employee ownership does not work well, an endowment (or endowments) could take a majority stake and guide in management, while still providing equity compensation to workers.

Whole-System Dynamics

Finally, we come to a consideration of the dynamics of the whole system of endowments. How will they relate to one another? Will there be any sort of governance, and if so, what could it be like?

The point that has been made consistently so far is that the civil endowment system will be decentralized. Another way to say this is that the governance style, if any, will not be based on legal authority or the imposition of central planning.

Instead, the endowments should take cooperation as their main mode of relationship. This, of course, is easy to say—and it may be dismissed as a naïve aspiration. Keep in mind, though, several things. First, the endowments will have a great deal of autonomy. They will not be required to cooperate in any particular way, but cooperation will be in their interest. The success of each individual endowment will be synergistic with the overall system. They will share knowledge and evolving "best practices."

An even more fundamental point about cooperation arises from the very nature of civil capital. If endowments live up to the definition of civil capital—that it is sourced voluntarily and endowed to all humanity—it follows logically that although these aggregations of wealth have independence, they are also in a real sense a part of a universal aggregation.

Endowments should make cooperation their main mode of relationship.

They don't have to be under central control to be that. For example, we don't have to realize that we are each part of the global ecosystem to be part of it. We are, whether we know it or not. Anyone who sincerely wanted to administer civil endowments would be conscious enough to recognize the value and necessity of cooperation, especially in light of what we're up against in terms of the entrenchment of power and habitual energy in the contemporary global economy. Ability to cooperate will be one of the survival skills of civil endowments, and it will be a big part of the appropriate oversight that will come from civil society generally and from the community of endowments. Endowments that cooperate well with other endowments will be deemed worthy of generosity and they will flourish.

If control is needed, it is in the realm of some sort of certification or feedback system for endowments. This is part of needed transparency and the overall reputation of civil capital. I am particularly concerned with the use of the term "civil endowment" (or whatever term comes to be standard). If the term is used willy-nilly by people who don't understand or respect the spirit of this innovation, it could be a very bad problem. Therefore, it is very likely that there will be some sort of effort at legal protection of the nomenclature associated with civil endowment. This is completely different than actually taking administrative control of endowments. The nomenclature could be overseen by a certifying agency controlling the use of a trademark, for example, restricting its use to endowments that meet certain standards. Eventually, I would hope there to be an ISO number for civil endowments.

Commons and Meta-Commons

It gets very exciting to envision the dynamics for the overall system of endowments when commons thinking is brought into the picture. The most basic element of a commons is a set of agreements among stakeholders as to how a "common pooled resource" (CPR) will be managed. As mentioned earlier, an individual endowment could possibly evolve its governance along commons lines. But as we look at the potential for a worldwide system of universal, local, and individual endowments, the idea of viewing and governing *the whole system* as a commons really stands out.

One way to look at it is that civil capital, by its very definition, is a common pooled resource. Although there can be any number of administrative bodies for such capital, the capital itself is a universal aggregation with the UB as its sole beneficiary.

Another way to conceptualize this is to view each endowment as a specific resource, and the whole system of endowments as the CPR. If each endowment is in some sense a commons, the universal assemblage of all the endowments could be called a meta-commons. Both these views are intriguing and they naturally lead to an inquiry as to how commons-style governance might be applied.

What follows is a brief look at Elinor Ostrom's eight design principles[2], and how they might be applied to a civil endowment system. The principles were derived from her meticulous fieldwork in observing traditional commons all over the world, and they represent a great deal of accumulated human wisdom. Whether or not we end up calling the civil endowment system a commons, we would ignore this wisdom at our peril. This is by no means a rigorous or complete application of Ostrom's principles, but it gives a preliminary glimpse as to how they might relate to the system.

PRINCIPLE 1: CLEARLY DEFINED BOUNDARIES

This principle refers to the definition of the CPR itself, and who has rights to it. In our case, it can be applied by agreeing on the very definition of civil capital and civil endowment organizations. By agreeing that civil capital is capital endowed to the perpetual common good of all humanity, a huge amount of clarity is achieved. Investments can be evaluated against this standard, as can the general behavior of an endowment.

---

2) Elinor Ostrom, *Governing the Commons*. New York, Cambridge University Press, 1990; p.88-103

As for the nature of endowment organizations, it can be agreed that they are NGOs, as opposed to for-profit entities, and that the behavior and compensation of people who work in them is subject to transparency and civil society oversight. The definition of the universal beneficiary is a clear boundary that points to the ultimate beneficial owner of all civil capital. There will be a great deal of creativity and flexibility possible within these boundaries, and keeping them intact will be immensely important in maintaining the integrity and potential of the system.

Principle 2: Congruence between appropriation and provisioning rules and local conditions

Ostrom found that a commons system that lasted over time used real-time information rather than rigid rules to determine who got what. Various forms of this principle will be helpful in shaping the dynamics of how endowments relate to each other. Within the system, there will be some kind of agreement that endowments will help each other. In particular, the older, larger, and richer endowments will try to contribute directly to newer, smaller, and less wealthy ones. However, the level of expectation involved needs to be flexible. If resources are invested as authentic civil capital, every investment will serve the common good. Newer organizations carry risk of failure. An endowment has good reasons for keeping its wealth, just as it does for giving it away.

There will also no doubt be considerable discussion as to where and how a particular endowment makes its investments. The application of this principle will be to ensure that such investments are made fairly among the various regions of the world, and that they are in accordance with emerging needs.

PRINCIPLE 3: COLLECTIVE CHOICE AGREEMENTS

Whereas the previous principle is essentially about finding appropriate rules, this one is more about participation in changing the rules. Ostrom observed that the people who are stakeholders in a commons need to take part in modifying rules and agreements when necessary. Effective change cannot be imposed from outside the system. The implication of this is that civil endowments would need to share a lot of information about how they govern themselves, and how they want to relate to other endowments, and their agreements would be constantly evolving.

PRINCIPLE 4: MONITORING

Ostrom points out that while managing the reputations of participants and fostering shared behavioral norms are important, that is not enough to create sustainable systems. Therefore, monitoring is necessary, and the key point she makes is that monitors are accountable to system members, or are chosen from among system members.

This speaks to the idea mentioned above of having a certifying agency that would function as a separate organization to keep track of endowments in both positive and negative ways. The agency would be a repository for best practices and spread the news about innovation, but it would also track deviations from the core principles of civil endowment. Endowments could also engage in monitoring other endowments as a community process.

The idea that monitors and system members are mutually accountable is absolutely crucial in the build-out of a civil endowment system worldwide. In particular, all parties would need to be committed to a respectful, responsive style of communication. The ultimate monitor of the system is civil society itself, and public opinion would not be kind if a community with such high ideals and lofty goals were to engage in quarrelsome behavior or petty disputes. To put it bluntly, we cannot afford to play hardball with each other.

The system will need to build itself very cautiously, with great appreciation for the interdependence of the public donor base, the various system members, and monitoring agencies. As mentioned, the existence of special foundations to help in the fundraising part of the process could be of great help, because these foundations would have to do their own monitoring in choosing endowments to fund, or to continue to fund.

PRINCIPLE 5: SANCTIONS

Ostrom's research showed that actual sanctions imposed on those who violated agreements in a commons came from within the system itself. In an extreme case, of course, a monitoring agency could publicly announce that it could no longer endorse an organization as a genuine civil endowment. This might have some effect, but the more powerful sanctions would come from loss of funding from other endowments and specialized foundations, loss of reputation in the endowment community, and very importantly, loss of opportunity to co-invest with other endowments.

The system will need to build itself very cautiously.

This last point refers to the real possibility that multiple endowments could take stakes in a particular project or investment, and thus mitigate their individual risk and increase their aggregate effectiveness in the economy. If an endowment came to be seen as a disreputable partner, the loss of such opportunities would be a very strong sanction indeed.

Principle 6: Conflict Resolution Mechanisms

In principle, the most potent approach to conflict is to avoid it in the first place. In a civil endowment system, the very independence of each endowment, along with the absence of central planning and authority, would create a structure in which conflict would be far less likely than in a top-down governance structure. It is more likely that conflict would come up with legal authorities or by way of outright political repression. In other words, conflict from outside the system is more to be expected than from within. In such cases, system members would need to react with solidarity and mutual aid. In the case of internal conflicts and disputes, it would be much better to resolve such problems internally, rather than through lawsuits and public vitriol. It would be in the interest of all system members to work in this way—perhaps through mediation, since the overall reputation of the system would be at issue, along with the reputations of individual parties to any conflict.

Principle 7: Minimal recognition of rights to organize

This principle brings us back to a point made very early in the book: that civil endowments depend on some level of basic open society. There is no doubt that governments could outlaw or otherwise impair the function of civil endowments. But given that we are discussing a transnational system here, at least some of the freedom that transnational corporations enjoy currently could apply to civil endowments. All governments are local. While it is true that a civil endowment could hardly be headquartered in every country of the world (North Korea comes to mind), multinational corporations (of which civil endowments would be in ownership positions) operate in many places in the world that are hostile to civil society organizations.

On the more positive side, there are plenty of countries that would be suitable ground for basing civil endowment organizations, as evidenced by the many large, powerful NGOs that exist in our world today. As the system develops, there will undoubtedly be legal struggles to gain more favorable political conditions for civil endowment, and there may be setbacks. In the end, the political climate may prove highly favorable to the system—at least in some places—which would enhance its activity and its prospects in other parts of the world. In the meantime, the operation of authentic civil capital will benefit everyone, across all borders.

Principle 8: Nested Enterprises

This design principle notes that the activities of complex commons systems take place in multiple layers of nested entities. Nothing could be closer than this to my vision of a system of universal, local, and individual endowments, all administered by autonomous NGOs operating in cooperation. All this activity would take place within an existing environment of local cultural practices, private enterprise, and governmental oversight. Ostrom notes that "all of the more complex, enduring CPRs meet this last design principle." The very appeal of civil endowment—and its very real chance for success—lies in the fact that it is specifically designed to function in this way, as a benign, nurturing force operating in a non-oppositional way with existing institutions.

As I have said, I am open to discussion as to just how linked this civil endowment idea will be with the emerging commons movement. I have no wish to co-opt or "enclose" this vibrant and immensely intelligent social force. To put it more bluntly, I have no desire to steal its ideas—or worse, warp and corrupt them. But the high degree of applicability to a system of civil endowments that I have found in the above eight principles bodes very well for some sort of healthy connection. Particularly at the global level, commons-style governance is an elegant fit—and opens up a realm of vast possibility.

The Exhortation

If we look at the economic challenges that face humanity, it is clear that we must explore new ways of thinking. If our contemplation is successful and new ideas emerge, to then make them meaningful, we must also take action in new ways. I assert that civil endowment is such an idea. Therefore, this Special Proposal is a specific call to action. To act at the scale and effectiveness we must achieve, we must build new kinds of institutions.

The fiduciary NGO as proposed here is such a new type of organization, and the overall proposed system of multiple NGOs linked in purpose and cooperation is also an innovation. It is important, though, to see that the basic work involved does not have to be invented out of whole cloth. There are organizations that operate in similar ways, such as public pension funds and the large endowments of private universities. Wealth management itself is a large and established field, with its own body of practical and theoretical knowledge and its own experienced professionals. Although civil endowment management is a new direction for fiduciary work, many of the needed human and theoretical resources are already in place.

The same is true when it comes to the aspirations of civil society activists and organizations. It is not as if there is no interest in economic transformation of the sort we have discussed, and which we will envision in more detail in the next chapter. There is abundant interest. I imagine that the leadership that comes forward in the management of civil endowments will be a vibrant mix of environmental and social activists, progressive business people, and financial sector professionals. The people are there, and the aspiration for a new direction is deeply rooted in society today. This part of the exhortation is to point out that *we can do this*.

The next part of the exhortation is to say that *we should do this*. I have never asserted that such a system will solve all human problems or bring about some sort of utopian outcome. But the ethical and compassionate basis of civil endowment is abundantly clear, as is its potential in the cause of economic justice. I assert that this is a worthy direction to embark upon, and that all of our efforts—from the smallest to the largest—will be beneficial.

Finally, it should also be clear that, given the urgency of human suffering and the looming environmental tipping points in areas such as climate change, we should start working on the implementation of the Special Proposal immediately. There are no obstacles to beginning right away, and therefore, *we should start now*.

This completes the exhortation, and with it, the Special Proposal.

CHAPTER EIGHT

The Transformation

IN THIS CHAPTER, WE WILL TAKE A LOOK AT HOW A CIVIL endowment system can function in a transformative way for human society. We will consider how it can enable a basic shift in the application of economic power, and then how that change relates to economic citizenship, to key processes such as investment and productivity, and to the very structure of the economy in the future. We will also give some thought to the fundamental problem of wealth inequality, and finally to the phases of development of the civil endowment movement. But first, let's look to the past, and explore the question of atonement.

The Economics of Atonement

Throughout history, we human beings have wronged each other in a stunning variety of ways, and the ongoing state of society is deeply burdened by that legacy. Are there ways we can address this fundamental problem—particularly in its economic dimensions? In short, is there an economics of atonement?

In the foregoing chapters we have discussed the merits of creating civil endowments as a remedy for our present and future economic ills. We are right to be concerned with sustainability, which is more or less about the future, and with economic injustice as it exists in the present. But these concerns are inevitably part of the cascading river of past human history that emerges in the present. And let's just say there's a lot of blood in the river.

I believe it is absolutely essential that we remedy injustices from the past, and that doing so is compassionate to those who have committed injustice as well as to those who have suffered it.

For example, take the case of some sort of toxic pollution that happened in the past. If we clean it up, the amount of harm it causes going forward will be greatly lessened. The person who made the mess is still responsible for the original indifference or ignorance involved, but it makes sense to me—intuitively at least—that if we mitigate the harm that person has caused, we will be helping them as well as those who are protected from that harm.

This is certainly true from a spiritual and karmic point of view. This sort of thinking can be extended to the vast range of injustices in human history. Even if you do not believe we can (or should) lessen the burden of those who have created harm, it definitely makes sense to unburden those who have suffered from it.

An interesting example of the wish to make things right is the behavior of the very rich in their support of charity and philanthropy. Reading the life stories of great "captains of industry" of the 19th century, such as J.P. Morgan and Andrew Carnegie, one is struck by the complexity and contradictions within their characters as they practiced philanthropy on a grand scale— with money earned by often-ruthless means. There is some evidence that Morgan and Carnegie viewed their philanthropy as atonement—at least in part—for their earlier actions. A critical view on this would be that the philanthropy of the rich does little to move society away from gross inequities of wealth and opportunity, and in fact perpetuates the system as it is, and business as usual.

My own view is not quite that severe, since the benefits of philanthropy are undeniable. If those efforts are in some regard self-serving for the philanthropist, well, they are human. And the rich are not solely responsible for reforming society, although many of them are trying to do so.

If we look honestly at the deep burden of injustice on a global scale throughout the whole arc of history—be it in the form of war, conquest, enslavement, exploitation, or environmental degradation—there is at least one thing we can do, and that is to form the intention of practicing economic atonement. Out of that intention may come some genuine action.

We are at a point in history where above all we need to recognize the inescapable oneness of the human family, and we need to see the responsibility that comes with seeing that fact. With all this in mind, I invite you to contemplate the totality of human experience—past, present, and future—and to consider how the heavy shadow of harm and injustice might be remedied.

One result that comes out of my own contemplation of this question is the idea of *atonement to the human whole*. If we see this need, and this possibility, we will see that practicing generosity toward the universal beneficiary is a very significant method of atonement in this way, because when we provide benefit to present and future generations, we are lessening the harm that past human actions have created. Therefore, this idea of universal atonement through the creation and operation of a civil endowment system is one response to the challenge of healing the wounds of the human family.

The tragedies of the past—in all their forms—are present in the continua of the individuals they affected in the past, but also in the psyche of each of us living today. Needless to say, this creates tremendous obstacles for all of us in the present and future.

If we can begin to resolve these heavy burdens on the human heart—or even forge new pathways for doing so—we will be doing quite a lot.

Reforming the Application of Capital's Power

We have seen that the workings of capital are the tangible manifestation of power in a modern economy. It follows that to change how such power manifests, we have to change how it is applied. Reptilian capital pursues the path of amoral wealth accumulation and maximization through enclosure, extraction, exploitation, and externalization. At a human level, reptilian capital divides people from each other, and cooperation is encouraged only when necessary to gain advantage over a common competitor. Even if we try to transcend these defects (and we must), we still must envision a realistic scenario for the operation of capital if we are to create a human future that is anything but catastrophic. We need capital because we need productivity.

I hope it has become clear by now that there is absolutely no reason or necessity, from the point of view of the nature and essence of capital, that it function in selfish and destructive ways. The movement toward the healthy functioning of capital has already been successfully undertaken in a preliminary way through the SRI movement, but that movement is simply too slow, too selective in its benefits, and too small in scale to make the differences that are needed. The movement toward forming civil capital and organizing it in endowments is a non-destructive innovation that will make all the existing aspects of an open-society economy function in more healthy ways. It is the quiet radicalism of the future.

The operation of civil capital is the direct antidote to the extremes of reptilian capitalism, and it is a fundamental improvement on the mammalian capitalism of SRI. Therefore, the first and most fundamental transformation we can point out regarding civil capital is that, by design, it is required to benefit all humanity—now and going forward. This is a transformation of economic power in the very basic sense that the efficacy of that capital is being applied to the common good of humanity.

The Transformation of Economic Citizenship

Our existing system features vast and catastrophic inequalities of wealth. Society is divided into the fortunate and the unfortunate, the powerful and the powerless, those who have sufficiency and those who do not, and those who exploit and those who are exploited. The conventional operation of capital is implicated in all these divisions. But so too is it responsible, broadly speaking, for rising standards of living worldwide, hope for personal betterment (in at least some countries), and the prospect of continuing innovation through technology of all kinds. It is easy to say that we simply need to throw away the bad stuff without getting rid of the good. However, it is not at all easy to do that, unless we create avenues for the reform of capital altogether.

There would be little hope for the improvement of economic citizenship if the model of *homo economicus,* in which rationality is solely devoted to the maximization of selfish desires, were the true and complete model of what it means to be human. Luckily, it is not. It is in fact an incomplete—and hence, inaccurate—model of human motivation, implemented for the convenience of economic thinkers who wanted to create simplistic explanations that would fit nicely into their equations and theories. In this regard, conventional economics—especially the entrenched neoclassical variety—is the poster child for ivory-tower hogwash.

A more complete and accurate model of economic motivation includes our pervasive capacity for cooperation, for kindness, and for sharing. This does not exclude looking out for our own interests, as well we should. Luckily, it is absolutely fine to have this complex mixture of qualities at play in the development of civil endowment. We do not need a world full of saints to make it happen. What we do need is to give people opportunities to structure their generosity in ways that extend to the universal whole. That is the first step, at least, in the transformation of economic citizenship.

New Possibilities for Productivity

In conventional thinking, the productivity of capital is considered to be financial profit. Actually, profit is merely an accounting quantity. It is a symbolic representation of productivity, and a rather arbitrary and incomplete one at that. The true measure of what capital "does" is its direct production of goods and services, along with related social and environmental effects. Financial results are just a piece of that picture.

Of course, productivity of tangible goods and services and the financial profit and loss associated with it are strongly coupled. However, that linkage is not linear in an actual production situation. Typically, the volume of production strongly affects profitability. What is at play is what is called the "marginal cost," which simply means the cost of the next unit of production.

In economies of scale, the marginal cost goes down as volume goes up. If enough can be sold at low enough marginal cost, that particular product will produce a financial profit. Civil capital could take advantage of the efficiencies of marginal cost in a different way. Production could be delivered through an entirely different channel than conventional markets, in the form of a direct production-credit system that would be allocated as a revenue-sharing vehicle.

How would this work? Remember that the universal beneficiary is designated as the owner of civil capital. This means that everyone has a right to be provided with a share of the productive output of the various investments. In conventional thinking, that would manifest itself as a dividend or income stream, i.e., a share of the profit. However, instead of (or in addition to) giving out cash royalties, the idea of using excess production capacity to deliver goods to people who really need them is quite intriguing.

Every person on Earth could have a production-credit account as a way of receiving their individual share of civil capital productivity. Firms financed with civil capital could fulfill their "cost of capital" obligations, at least in part, by producing extra goods (at reduced marginal cost) and making those goods available for production credits, which could be allocated on a need basis to people at the low end of the income scale.

I'm thinking for example, of a factory in China that might sometimes have excess capacity, and people in, say, Africa, who have terrible shortages of basic goods. This could create a win-win situation. Whereas goods sold on the open market have marketing expenses and face uncertain demand, this category of low marginal-cost goods could take advantage of extra capacity when available and be delivered into specialized distribution channels for direct provisioning. Low marginal cost does not mean "low quality." The production-credit goods would be part of standard production, not special goods for charity. The transport and delivery of such goods would provide additional jobs and entrepreneurial opportunities in developing economies.

The key point in all this is that firms would be able to make use of the efficiency of lower marginal cost of production to fulfill their obligations while also fulfilling real needs for the poor. What is happening here is twofold: the firm is able to monetize production that it could not sell on the open market. The goods are provided as a dividend of civil capital to those who cannot afford them, so there is no negative impact on sales. The return to the firm would be accounted for in terms of either repaying what is effectively interest on the capitalization of the firm, or fulfilling a royalty agreement built into being a civil endowment financed company. The benefit to the firm would be that it would be able to fulfill these obligations with goods made at low marginal cost—production that would otherwise not even happen in a pure market situation.

The potential of this sort of idea may be a bit hard to grasp at first, since we are habituated to thinking in terms of an exchange economy that supposedly follows the laws of the market. Anyone who looks accurately at markets, however, realizes that they are deeply flawed in practice and are subject to all sorts of distortions. In particular, markets don't address—let alone solve—the problem of poverty. The mechanism described here *does* address poverty in a very real way. This system could function alongside conventional market structures and provide real benefits in addressing the wealth divide.

Transforming Investment

In the Special Proposal, we saw in some detail the kinds of structures and organizational processes that would be involved with the work of civil endowments. This is the first and most important aspect of the transformation of investment, since it creates a set of conditions in which the kinds of investment decisions appropriate to the universal beneficiary can be made. I don't wish to pre-define the sorts of investment vehicles that might be used, since that would be the job of the decision makers in the various organizations. It should be understood that ownership of even very commonplace types of equities by the universal beneficiary would represent a transformative state of affairs. However, there are a few possibilities in terms of investment types that might be mentioned here.

The first of these possibilities is the funding of worker cooperatives. It should be understood, of course, that the normal state of affairs with this type of entity is for the workers themselves to provide the capital. In practice, however, the prospects of worker cooperatives could be greatly enhanced by having readily available and "friendly" financing available at startup, which could then be paid back by the workers on favorable terms over time.

Another very strong possibility for leveraging the benefits of civil capital would be to invest in community capital organizations. Although there are several meanings for the term "community capital"—some are basically government-sourced loan funds, used primarily for low-income housing—the meaning I'd like to use here is more along the lines of localized community inputs of savings and retirement funds for local investment. In other words, local people put up money to be invested locally. The value of such organizations, like that of worker cooperatives, is in the empowerment of ordinary people acting on their own home ground to build an economy that they themselves help define, and from which they will benefit. As with worker cooperatives, such projects could receive a very strong boost from civil endowments taking an initial stake in such a fund, which the community could buy out over time.

Finally, there is one prospective type of investment vehicle that would come into possibility by virtue of the very existence of civil endowments. These could be called "parallel funds." The idea here is that civil endowments would change the risk profile of the socially and environmentally progressive equities in which they invest, and create favorable opportunities for private investors to participate in those same investments. In other words, the strength of the civil endowment would make a whole new set of mutual fund opportunities open up, using the same investment protocols as a civil endowment. This would in effect be another type of—or enhancement of—the prospects of socially responsible investing. Parallel funds could operate alongside civil endowments with excellent synergistic effect.

Transforming the Tangible Economy

In all the areas we will discuss briefly below, civil investment will create a multi-dimensional effect. If, for example, we channel investment toward more ecologically friendly enterprises, that is in itself a good thing. But a civil investment also broadens ownership distribution in absolutely everything it does. Even giving one penny to an endowment increases the effective capitalization of everyone on the planet—albeit by an infinitesimal amount. Civil-funded firms will be structured to shift ownership to employees and pay a balanced spread of salaries.

Let's look first at three of biggest issues of our time: climate change, extreme poverty, and wealth inequality. It is pointless to try to decide whether the issue of climate change is more or less important than severe poverty and starvation. That is some kind of "Sophie's Choice" that we simply don't have to debate. With multiple endowments and types of endowments, the movement will address these issues in synergistic ways. Some endowments will focus on energy, some on agriculture, and so on. Although I'm starting with climate change, don't think I am forgetting that right now as I write this, someone is starving to death.

It is encouraging to see, as of this writing in early summer 2015, the really robust development of renewable energy worldwide. Certain amazing facts are popping up, like the fact that on certain days Scotland is producing more than 100 percent of its electricity needs with wind. Germany has had similar short periods recently of combined wind/solar generation. It is now looking like we could really turn the corner on phasing out fossil fuels.

Giving one penny to an endowment increases the effective capitalization of everyone on the planet.

At the same time, of course, oil and gas extraction is booming in the United States, and we have become the world's top producer in both categories. Russia remains vastly dependent on its fossil-fuel production. Thus, there are signs of promise, but we certainly are not out of the woods. As the world shifts its energy production to renewables, two questions emerge: (1) will we do it fast enough to stave off catastrophic warming? And, (2) when the changeover happens, who will own it?

Moving massive capital investment into renewables through civil endowments could provide positive outcomes in regard to both these questions. We still need to see tipping points and shifts of momentum. Some of the obstacles are political of course, but time is of the essence, and the populist dimension of civil endowments will provide impetus at many levels beyond just the financial.

The same is true from the point of view of ownership. At this point (as is true with all large-scale capital projects) the owners of any sort of energy production project leverage vast amounts of loaned money into equity and profit. This is true whether it is a wind farm or a fracking well. The ecological implications are different, of course—but the financial ones, not so much. As we've seen, civil capital has a completely different life cycle, and whether finance capital is provided as loans or equity, the proceeds go to the universal beneficiary. Energy production is also an excellent prospect for the kind of production credit system described above. There is no reason that a local endowment could not fund and own a wind farm, and put part of the produced electricity into such a system from which it could be directly provisioned as royalties. Some local governments are doing something just like that now in the Western United States, although they sell the electricity on the open market and send residents a check each year.

Renewable energy is a great example of low marginal cost, since once the equipment is installed, it has a projected lifespan wherein further production costs are quite low—compared to continuously having to feed a coal plant, for example. I believe this fact and the less centralized nature of solar and wind generation lend themselves very well to civil endowment investment. I hope that civil endowments will be strong leaders in creating the needed tipping points of scale that are so vitally needed for our shared energy future. Concerning extreme poverty and malnutrition internationally, it would be very naïve to say that a civil endowment system could quickly turn the situation around completely. That would assume that there are quick fixes in this area—and there are not. According to data from Oxfam, as of around 1970, over 30 percent of the world's population was undernourished. This figure fell steadily to about 16 percent in 2005, but then has been rising ever since, to around 20 percent. There are now close to one billion people who are considered malnourished, a condition that contributes to the deaths of 3.1 million children under age five per year, or about one every 10 seconds.

It is very hard to write these things and then say, "Well, things were worse, percentage-wise, in 1970." It doesn't matter. The situation of poverty and hunger in our world is an outrage, and if paying even minimal attention to it doesn't make us want to change things very fundamentally, I don't know what will. How could civil endowment help? The very nature of civil capital is that it is an equity holding for everyone on Earth. If we establish an endowment, everyone has an asset stake, however small. And everyone has a claim on production from those investments. This could apply to food and medicine as well as it could to electricity or shoes.

It is important to see that universal sufficiency in food (which is only part of sufficiency, but obviously a crucial one) is not a huge matter in terms of the absolute magnitude of global wealth. It is commonly believed that we produce enough food in the world today to feed everybody. The problems are in distribution, and quite literally in people having the money to buy it. The existence of civil endowment creates a fundamental shift in the second of these problems, by establishing a universal claim—however modest at first—on productivity. It is a claim created not by law but by human decency arising from civil society.

I do not pretend to lay out a definite plan around global hunger and extreme poverty here. Perhaps a first step would be to contribute food from civil-funded agriculture for distribution through NGO channels. As well, many NGOs are also doing entrepreneurial support in developing economies. Civil endowment financial institutions could get involved. Microloans have been an important innovation in the developing world, but they are also subject to abuses and limitations.

What might be the next step beyond microloans? Perhaps it could be simple grants from large endowments in the developed world to responsible local parties in impoverished places so they can create their own endowments. Those endowments could then buy farmland and find ways to transition it to egalitarian ownership of family farm holdings (or cooperative ventures) over time. Money paid to buy such farms would go back to the local endowment, not outside investors. All these ideas are just sketches, and their scope very much depends on the overall scale of the civil endowment system. But in the short term, pilot programs developed in cooperation with local governments and established aid NGOs could show the way forward.

In the most general sense, the operation of civil endowment could also bring social and political benefits by encouraging innovation and open society in places where cultural inertia impedes change. If the overall system gets large enough, it could have a huge effect on eliminating poverty altogether.

As we contemplate the big issues around hunger, agriculture, and climate change, we see how interrelated they are. One thing that jumps out is the large contribution of agriculture to greenhouse gas emissions. Agriculture alone has been estimated at about 14 percent of this total, but then if we consider deforestation (which is often for agriculture) that adds in another 18 percent.

The contribution of animal husbandry to this total is very large, since cattle especially give off large amounts of methane, a greenhouse gas far more damaging than carbon dioxide. One implication of this is that vegetarian food production will be extremely important for the future, in addition to humanitarian concerns.

Since people both need and crave protein, meat-substitute enterprises would be a very interesting avenue of investment. And since weather patterns are increasingly unpredictable due to climate change, indoor farming—be it traditional greenhouse operations or more high-tech "vertical farm" operations—could become vitally important too. In all this, the role of innovation is one that civil capital can and should take up. Really living up to its long-term game plan would require no less.

To consider all the ways that civil endowments could participate and benefit the tangible economy going forward would require a whole book in itself. The very brevity of my discussion here is in consideration of that, but also in recognition that the journey of imagination that civil endowment will create is not just for my mind alone, but for many minds, stretching far into the future.

Wealth Inequality

The general issue of wealth inequality (as distinct from absolute poverty) is again very complex, but in this case too, civil endowment is a slow—but fundamental—remedy. The very DNA of civil capital is egalitarian, and committed to allowing people to be lifted up in sufficiency and opportunity.

If we are to respect the meticulous research of Thomas Piketty in his recently famous book *Capital in the 21st Century*, it is not just the present situation of wildly unequal wealth that we should be worried about, but the future trend as well. He believes that the concentration of wealth into large private fortunes is a systemic feature of our present-day economic system, and that we are headed for more, not less inequality. Piketty's suggested solution to this problem—taxation of accumulated wealth (in addition to income)—is, by his own admission, fraught with difficulties.

Wealth is far too mobile today to make this proposal work out without ironclad international agreements and unified action by just about all the national governments.

Civil endowment takes an entirely different approach to this issue—by starting from the bottom up. Every bit of wealth given into the civil endowment system is a de facto adjustment of wealth inequality, since it is endowed equally to all. If this were simply static wealth, its effects would not be very impressive, and certainly not very fast acting. But the wealth of civil endowment is not static; it is capital. By creating civil capital, we are initiating an economic process which is, by design, intended to build wealth in egalitarian ways, and especially to lift up those at the lower end of the scale.

Most of the great fortunes we see today have been built on capital gains that translate to highly concentrated business assets. The productivity and capital gains arising from the civil endowment system will have an entirely different arc, as I hope I've made clear by now. It may seem intuitively useful to attempt to adjust wealth inequality by taking wealth from the rich. However, and aside from the fact that, realistically speaking, the rich are pretty darned good at holding on to their wealth, it is time to start thinking about building new wealth and spreading it more fairly. This is the approach of civil endowment.

The problem with great concentrations of wealth is not simply that the very rich have so much. It is that they use it in so many ways that are harmful to the rest of us. This includes, of course, their inordinate exercise of political power. The great fossil-fuel fortunes come to mind as outstanding examples of that. While civil endowments are not intended specifically as political power centers, they will be large aggregations of wealth, and will have influence where appropriate, especially in economic decision making. The example of the large philanthropic NGOs today indicates that big chunks of money can get things done around big problems.

In the end, we may also find that the very rich—or at least a sizable slice of that group—may become great friends of the civil endowment movement. This will in part hinge on the question of tax deductions for contributions to endowments. If there is a movement in keeping with Piketty's suggestions to appropriate wealth from large fortunes (or even if there is not), the business-minded rich may find it entirely more palatable to give money to endowments for direct economic development than to give it to governments for bureaucrats to spend. Indeed, who understands capital better than the rich? If they find it to their liking, they will find ways to dodge government appropriation and put their money to far better use as civil capital. Civil endowment may eventually become the ultimate philanthropy.

That possibility being as it may, it is still not the best—and should certainly not be the only—hope for robust growth of the movement. Putting our hopes on the rich is entirely the wrong orientation that is needed. We need to grow civil endowment from the bottom, from the middle, *and* from the top of the wealth scale. Indeed, many of us who are toward the middle or lower end of wealth in rich countries are still vastly better off than the bottom two billion or so of humanity. The implication of that is that what we can contribute can be very significant in a global context. I also think, speaking from a karmic point of view, that the more impoverished a person may be, the more significant even a tiny, symbolic contribution to civil capital may be in raising consciousness and engendering human solidarity and hope.

The Phases of Civil Endowment

How do we reconcile the idea that civil endowment is a worthy endeavor at any level of scale with the prospect that it can become a major factor in a positive economic future of mankind? In other words, how might it develop? In contemplating this question, I envision three major phases: namely, the symbolic, catalytic, and structural phases, which describe the potential process of development and transformation of the system.

In the symbolic phase, the main benefit is in the communication of the very possibility of civil endowment, and in the establishment of the necessary institutions for its operation. In the next, catalytic phase, civil endowment gains very real economic power, and is able to leverage various tipping points and gain substantial support. Finally, in the structural phase, it takes its place in a large-scale way as a foundation of a healthy world economy.

The symbolic phase starts from zero, in the first act of giving to an endowment. In that sense, every contributor to civil endowment will go through the symbolic phase as they enter into the understanding of it, resolve to make a contribution, and then do so. This contribution could be in the form of money or of some kind of work. It is interesting to imagine various ways that this could happen. Perhaps in the future, when the whole system is well established, young people will make a very small contribution of money they earned themselves as part of a ceremony, a rite of passage into adulthood and entry into a consciousness of global human solidarity.

Another interesting idea would be to have a kiosk in a public place with a stationary bike attached to a generator, which feeds into the grid. People could stop in and pedal for a while, and their contribution of human energy could be recorded as a donation to civil capital. This would also be quite educational, of course, in regard to the amount of electricity we use, and its financial value in relation to the energy output of a human being.

I am going to set forth some admittedly arbitrary milestones for these phases, just to give a sense of quantitative reference points. More important than the actual financial figures is the description of what would be established in reaching each of these stages. The numerical milestones mentioned will give an idea of a goal for the accomplishment of that phase.

The symbolic phase, as I've said, starts at zero. As for the criteria for the achievement of this phase, I would like to set a goal of creating at least one functioning endowment with a value of one U.S. penny for each human being on the planet. As of this writing, the global population is about 7.2 billion, which means the Penny Endowment would have a target value of roughly 72 million dollars. To create an endowment of this size there would have to be a well-run non-profit fiduciary organization, as well as an ongoing process for the investment of the money.

This goal of a penny per capita sums up the symbolic phase of civil capital. At some level it seems easy to envision. It brings up thoughts like, "why couldn't permanently endowing such a small amount to each human being be possible?" But of course, the total amount is not trivial. Therefore, the whole endeavor would represent a fairly significant accomplishment involving many people and a good deal of organizational development. The existence of the Penny Fund would also drive a lot of discussion about how it should be invested. It would bring public awareness. The operation of such an amount of money in the global economy might be considered negligible, but the very existence of a functioning endowment would be very significant.

The catalytic phase would start from there. I would like to set a rough milestone for accomplishment of this phase at a total of 100 billion dollars, which is around 14 dollars per capita. This number is set in part because it is a nice round number that is significantly larger than the fortunes of the world's richest men, which currently peak at just under $80 billion. We typically think of the world's richest people as very powerful, and indeed they are. I think it would be an interesting milestone for the universal beneficiary to reach and surpass that level.

More important, however, for the catalytic phase would be the expansion of the system into any number of vibrant endowments, capable of not only significant direct investment, but also of exercising activist investor clout in the realm of publicly traded corporations. Also characteristic of this phase would be the establish-

The Penny Endowment would have a target value of roughly 72 million dollars.

ment of at least one civil endowment foundation, which could greatly accelerate fundraising and channel funds to new and existing endowments—while exercising a degree of oversight through the power of the purse. As well, this level of capitalization would enable the outright ownership of various kinds of financial institutions, including retail and investment banks, community capital organizations, and the like.

In chemistry, a catalyst is a substance that creates conditions for certain desired reactions, without actually being consumed in those reactions. The implication of the use of this term here is that even at the level of 100 billion dollars in value, the civil endowment system would not be a huge player in the world economy, although it certainly could go beyond the symbolic level and catalyze some positive and inspiring changes. It could leverage innovation and exercise leadership far beyond what its size might suggest.

Finally, the structural level is where civil endowment would truly come into its own. In this phase, there would be a full range of universal, local, and individual endowments. Alternative financial institutions would expand and flourish, as would the influence of civil capital in conventional global markets. A production credit system would become operational, which would make significant inroads on poverty while lowering unemployment in developed economies. The development of structuralized inputs would need to be very strong at this point.

At this level, I also hope we could see significant progress in obtaining universal resource royalty rights, along with the understanding that civil endowments are the best recipients for such flows, so that they can leverage prosperity on an egalitarian basis for the indefinite future. Ideally, such progress would parallel the emergence of a global commons movement that could eventually bring about a truly healthy relationship between humanity and the natural world. At that point, civil capital would be understood and governed as a commons, alongside a globally established natural commons of the atmosphere, the seas, and natural resources.

I would like to set a milestone of 1,000 dollars per capita for this structural phase. This is something of an arbitrary figure, but it brings up some quantitative thinking for comparison. At current population levels, that would amount to a total value of combined endowments of over seven trillion dollars. This may seem like an unattainable number. But if we compare it to the size of the overall world economy, and think about a realistic time frame, it starts to seem less farfetched. In 2014, the estimated overall amount of global economic activity, expressed in terms of purchasing power, was more than 100 trillion dollars. Global assets have been estimated at 240 trillion dollars.

We should understand that a goal of 1,000 dollars per capita is something that could be accomplished, say, in a generation, with a combination of many inputs. How could we reach this basic structural level in 20 years? Simple arithmetic shows that inputs of 50 dollars per year per capita would come to 1,000 dollars in that time. Although conventional fundraising will be significant during the symbolic and catalytic phases of the system, it is both unlikely and unnecessary that a structural level would be reached in that way. Instead, it can come from a combination of structuralized inputs, such as natural resource royalties (including carbon taxes or fees), fees from financial transactions such as currency exchange, and revenue sharing from companies aligned with the civil endowment mission.

Building out a civil endowment system will be a tricky process, and it is admittedly speculative to talk in terms of specific details of its long-term success. Nevertheless, its transformative potential is very real. Considering the dangers that we all face in an uncertain future, and the prospect such a system embodies for promoting human wellbeing and opportunity, it is eminently worth our best efforts to bring it into manifestation.

CHAPTER NINE

The Special Economics of Compassion

W E NOW TURN BACK TO THE ECONOMICS OF COMPASSION, and look at how the six virtues set forth in Chapter Three can be applied specifically to the work of civil endowment. The six virtues—generosity, ethics, non-aggression, diligence, focus, and wisdom—constitute a general economics of compassion. They are valuable and applicable to economic matters across the board. Here, we bring them to bear on the specific subject matter of this book, and examine a special economics of compassion, which will provide a summary and conclusion to our journey of thought.

Generosity

Generosity is the pragmatic foundation of the civil endowment idea. It is what moves it from pure theory—or even fantasy—to workable, feasible practice. The whole notion that capital could be perfected—that it could work in a fully compassionate way for the common good—is wonderful, but it is utterly impractical if there is no way for such capital to come into existence. The fact that generosity can be the practical seed of it all is what allows us to talk about this as a real possibility.

Generosity provides the basic purification of provenance that makes civil capital possible. What is meant by this is that the conventional sources of wealth used to form capital are morally encumbered by how that wealth was obtained, and especially by the intentions behind the process. Even in the case of honest business dealings, there is the intention to gain profit for the investor, and to do so within a limited time frame. Especially if the intentions behind private investment are in fact honest, there is no inherent fault with private investment. The only problem is that it is utterly impossible to create economic justice for all with an economy that relies on purely private investment.

To understand why this is so, let us look at economic transfers at a very basic level. There are three kinds: reciprocal exchanges, theft or coercion, and gifts. Some kinds of transfers, such as taxes, can be considered borderline or "grey-area" cases. But generally, exchanges fall into these categories, or variants of them. Nearly all economic theory is concerned with the analysis of reciprocal exchanges. However, there is no real way that an economy based only on reciprocal exchanges can lead to justice,

There is no way that an economy based only on reciprocal exchanges can lead to justice.

simply because there has never been a fair starting point for economic wealth and power. You can't start with a rigged, unbalanced game, and then say, "Let's play by these nice, fair rules."

This might sound like an argument for socialist appropriation, but it is not. I believe the evidence of history shows that economic administration based on centralized governmental authority is fundamentally flawed. It is also true that getting back property that has been unfairly appropriated—whether it is by conquest, exploitation, or simple capital gains—is a vastly complicated and messy matter. The fact that such ownership is morally tainted does not point to a simple resolution. The only fundamental way to break the cycle is through the gift economy.

CIVIL ENDOWMENT

Therefore, even though simply gifting wealth to civil capital may seem idealistic or far-fetched, it is actually a pragmatic, real-world way to move toward economic justice. As we have discussed, the will to justice is always, and must be, based on some level of compassion. Why would we want fairness for all if we had no concern and respect for all? Therefore, we should acknowledge our compassion, own it, and go with it!

Generosity does not have to be romanticized or even spiritualized. It can be ordinary and routine. However, the heart-level engagement can also be very deep. I'm thinking of people who give their own blood, or who donate organs or bone marrow. This human inclination to give is very profound. One of the most touching moments (for me at least) in all of literature is the famous scene at the end of John Steinbeck's *The Grapes of Wrath*. An impoverished family of refugees from the Dust Bowl comes upon a stranger, an emaciated old man who is literally dying of hunger. A young nursing mother takes him to her breast and feeds him with her own milk, and that is where the book ends. This expression of the deepest level of human kindness is emblematic of the kind of redemption and transformation that generosity brings, and of its necessity. It is literally the hope of humanity.

As for my own hopes, I do aspire that a significant number of people will understand this in regard to civil endowment. It is very important that large numbers of people give small, token amounts, to connect themselves with this movement and find a way forward. I also hope that some among the very wealthy will give especially large, inspiring donations. As we move forward, and find ways to voluntarily embed tiny deductions from many types of financial transfers, the generosity of funding civil endowment will become effortless.

Ethics

We could describe civil endowment very simply by saying that it has the purpose of creating truly ethical investments on a very large scale. Therefore, this ethical intention is the operational foundation of the idea. As we have seen, for this to work, the ownership and administration of civil capital must be detached from egoistic concerns. Even the most legitimate of selfish concerns, such as simply providing for oneself and family, means putting on blinders. People must be allowed to take care of themselves, but we must go further. In particular, the concern for future generations that is built into civil capital is the expression of the ethical leap we could, and must, make.

All of this creates unprecedented challenges in decision making for those guiding civil investment. The subtleties and nuances of the investment calculus and the portfolio theory for this work can scarcely be known to me today as I write this. Such a body of knowledge and discipline can only come from shared experience—from successes, failures, and the wisdom of many good minds. What we *can* say definitively, though, is that the ethical foundations of the system can be expressed. They are grounded in non-exclusion—in universal, whole-system, unbounded concern. If real compassion is unbiased compassion, we can follow its implications all the way to a vision of universal economic justice. That is the unshakeable foundation on which we can stand.

At the same time, though, we must not be rigid. The fact that we don't *need* to be rigid speaks to the amazing flexibility that the civil endowment idea embodies. We can implement justice at whatever level of scale mankind's generosity permits. We do not have to force any ideas on people. As universal and profound as the ethical dimension of this idea may be, being non-dogmatic about it is essential. Trying to force ideas on people can lead them to just reject those ideas out of hand. Therefore, we must be very careful in the process of communicating our moral idealism, and simply put it into practice.

Non-Aggression

If ethics is the operational foundation of the civil endowment work, then non-aggression is its psychological foundation. It is the attitude we have to have, and the policy we have to follow. To extend the discussion above about how to communicate ideas of the system, it seems clear that we have to use non-aggressive methods and language. If this whole system is based on compassion, our very way of working must honor that fact.

As was said in the earlier chapter on the general economics of compassion, this quality of non-aggression, which can also be called tolerance or forbearance, is what makes cooperation possible. Think about how important cooperation is going to be in building a civil endowment system.

Cooperation is the survival trait that makes human life and human society possible. We don't have poison fangs or huge teeth or armor shells. We evolved with soft skin, dexterous hands, and high intelligence. Now, at this time in history, we have to use our uniquely human qualities to make the kinds of changes needed for human society to survive another set of challenges. They are challenges of remarkable complexity on a global scale, but addressing them comes down to actions we can all take, and to shifts in our attitudes that will influence not just our own states of mind, but those around us, and those with whom we interact—whether they are next door or on the next continent. It bears repeating that non-aggression makes cooperation possible, because cooperation makes everything possible.

Those who work for civil endowment will have to practice tolerance in many ways. You may have to practice tolerance for ridicule and dismissal of your work. You will have to grapple with the idea that universal endowments mean you are benefitting people who may not like you. Some people may be suspicious of everything you do; and you, in turn, may not like them very much sometimes. People will also say, "Well, does that mean we are giving wealth to murderers and terrorists?" You will have to think about questions like that.

We will also have to find tolerance and patience for failure when it happens, for criticism that goes beyond mere dismissal, for disharmony in our organizations, and possibly, for political repression. Staying with non-aggression in all these sorts of circumstances will be up to us as individuals, and probably very challenging. It strengthens my heart to think about the strong examples of non-violent social activism that we see in history and in present times. I feel a sense of inspiration that our economic activism could take its place in that history.

Diligence

The application of diligence to civil endowment is simple but profound. If we give some of our wealth to an endowment, it means we have spent the time and effort that it took to acquire that wealth working for all humanity. We have put our shoulders to the wheels of atonement, of sufficiency, of opportunity, and of transformation. Therefore, our diligence is most appropriate. For many, this profound but easy gift will be their diligence.

For others, it could take many forms. NGOs typically function with a mixture of volunteer and professional workers. Chances are that a lot of the hard labor in founding endowments will be done free of charge by activists. Financial professionals will no doubt earn less than those who go down the crazy salary/bonus rat race of Wall Street. CEOs of civil funded companies will not get salaries 331 times that of ordinary staff.[1] These sacrifices could be seen as generosity, but also as diligence in the sense of actually working for a reasonable wage— of earning one's money.

There is also the diligence of study, of reflection, and of pondering and debating the calculus of investment decision making. This isn't going to be altogether easy. There will be roadblocks in the work along with the breakthroughs. The same goes without saying for fundraising for endowments. If we are willing to give whatever effort it takes to build the system, then that is diligence. If we go to another level and take the leap that makes it inspiring and fun, then we will fulfill the Buddhist definition of diligence, which is "taking joy in virtue."

Focus

Thinking back to what was said in Chapter Three, you will recall that focusing is a psychological practice that brings our experience into clarity and stability, and that responsible decision making requires effective focusing as a basis. I would like to emphasize the ramifications of that idea as we consider how it applies specifically to civil endowment work. Throughout the forgoing chapters, especially "The Special Proposal," we have discussed the significance of

---

1) This is the most recent statistic I've seen on that particular wealth divide for Fortune 500 companies in the United States.

organizational structure and functioning quite extensively, as well as the all-important investment calculus at the heart of the work of endowment organizations. It was also noted earlier that the outcome of focusing is "refinement." These are important points to bring together.

The work of focusing in regard to civil endowment is going to be ongoing. It is not just about chewing on a question and coming up with "the answer." The answer is more about the process, and the process involves continuously bringing the right questions, the right intellectual resources, and the right skills into play. That is when we will have responsible decision making for the universal beneficiary. In that way, focusing becomes a transpersonal process, one of ongoing learning. The evolution of the portfolio theory, the protocols, the organizational norms, and all other aspects of civil endowment theory is the essence of the work at the highest level of policy leadership. It all depends on effective focusing.

Another aspect of the challenge here is to find effective ways to communicate and connect the civil endowment ideas with other positive movements in society today. This includes leaders and groups around the environment, the commons, gender-related justice, indigenous people, and spiritual traditions. Eventually, it also means connecting with—and inspiring—members of the power elites who have so much influence in our world. This is not just about finding language and talking points. It is about discovering real human resonance. It requires penetration into whatever areas of genuine shared values are there.

This whole notion of mental penetration speaks also to understanding some of the more difficult aspects and ramifications of civil endowment theory. For example, I've mentioned the notion of an "efficiency of universal scope." This idea took a long time to arise in my own mind, and I am still in a process of reflection and inquiry toward seeing the full extent of its implications.

The same point applies to the marginal-cost efficiencies that could make a production credit system so powerful. I really believe people—and not just wonky economics specialists—can understand these things. But that will take focused consideration, and maybe coming back for another pass at a later time. If you are familiar with meditation practice, you know that one key method is "returning again and again" to the focus.

In the most general sense, the application of the virtue of focusing to civil endowment is to keep it in mind, and to let your understanding and inspiration grow through continued attention. If enough people do that, it will take root and make a very big difference. That is my aspiration.

Wisdom

Finally, let's think about economic wisdom in relation to civil endowment. This theory itself is an expression of my long-term search for wisdom in this field, and by that I do not just mean some sort of high-minded theory. In economics, wisdom requires practicality. Although the content of this theory is unusual and unconventional, it is actually practical. It could be put into play in society, starting now. Sadly, most conventional theories of economics are actually very utopian, even if they are entrenched in our consciousness. That is why a lot of discussion on the topic is just fruitless contestation—and humanity suffers the consequences. Obviously, the determination of whether this civil endowment idea is really an expression of wisdom—or merely the drivel of an idealistic dreamer—is not mine to make. But either way, it is offered for your consideration.

Post-Materialism

In the general sense, we saw that post-materialism as a foundation of economic wisdom comes down to psychological non-attachment to the coarse level of appearances, to selfishness, and to quantitative notions of wealth. How does that apply to the specific context of civil endowment? Fundamentally, we can say that it means to conduct a process of investment using an overarching, positive set of human values as the guiding principle. In

Although civil endowment theory is unconventional, it is actually practical.

practice, it means that investment does not operate out of an extractive or exploitive mindset, but rather one of universal productivity. Therefore—and although it may be counterintuitive to say so—post-materialist investment is not at all inimical to prosperity.

Another meaning of post-materialism in this context relates to the product philosophy implicit in the operation of civil capital. This can be summarized with the idea of "transcending frivolity." If we put the usefulness of a product first, we will discover a whole sense of direction in product design that takes us past our present age of waste and superficiality and built-in obsolescence.

Ironically, this will lead us to greater respect for materiality in the conventional sense of the world. Getting past psychological materialism, which is a sick, superficial, and addictive relationship with materiality, and which leads to the throwaway mentality and endless waste of material and energy, will take us to a new era of resourceful and respectful relations with the material world.[2]

---

2) For an inspiring look at this topic, see *The Upcycle: Beyond Sustainability—Designing for Abundance*, by William McDonough and Michael Braungart (New York: North Point Press, 2013).

Finally, going beyond psychological materialism pertains to our thinking and to getting past conventional truths. If we are able to go beyond our conceptual entrenchment—attachment to our very ideas—we enter into a very creative space of open possibilities. Of course, letting go of conventional thinking could also yield up a lot of wild and useless ideas—and no doubt the present theory will be labeled as such by some! In any case, it is important to let go of attachment to ideas, even if they are valid.

As we saw in the application of non-aggression to communicating the civil endowment idea, pressing ahead in a dogmatic way is simply not effective. It is not a good strategy. And here, at the level of wisdom, our freedom from dogma goes beyond that, because in the best case it is a freedom from fixation on our conceptual constructs altogether. Although this may seem rather esoteric, it is also down to earth. It is better not to be so sure of ourselves, and better to listen to what people have to say, and to think about it. If we have confidence in our ideas and aspirations, they will keep their integrity without a lot of grasping and struggle.

Freedom of thought lets us go beyond the "presumption of greed" that underlies conventional capital theory, and lets us see that the spirit of capital could be perfected. We could also see that the kind of security that a civil endowment system could provide will allow people to behave much better than they do now—to live in a state of greater solidarity with one another, and to focus more on quality of life. The compassionate spirit of this system can lead us away from conflict, wastefulness, and even laziness. This all comes from freeing ourselves from materialism. Therefore, it is very important to do so.

Co-Centricity

The co-centric wisdom should be understood as the completion of wisdom, in the sense the co-centricity and post-materialism are in and of themselves co-centric. I hope that formulation is not seen as some kind of sophistry. What it really means is that there are not two wisdoms, but that we can express the idea of economic wisdom in these two broad categories. As was discussed earlier, post-materialism pertains to refuting and moving past our misconceptions of how things are, and co-centricity is an expression of how things *really* are. Practically speaking, you can't have one without the other.

In particular, co-centric wisdom means working with authentic whole-system thinking, and seeing pervasive interdependence as "the way things work." This is the basis of the investment logic for civil endowments. Co-centricity can also be understood as rigorous non-exclusion. The main expression of this is a social one: non-exclusion means universal inclusion. Nobody is left out, and certainly not future generations. Non-exclusion also means, of course, the natural environment of our Earth. Putting this all into practice in an ongoing way with this whole system is the essence of civil endowment theory.

Finally, at the inner level, the level of the heart, the essence of co-centricity is compassion itself. And here, we come full circle. The basic compassion that lies behind all six virtues comes to completion through being fully stabilized in our hearts and minds in wisdom. We can build this co-centric wisdom into the social and economic systems that we create. That is the extraordinary potential of civil endowment.

* * *

Afterword

THIS BOOK IS NOT JUST A SYSTEM OF IDEAS—IT IS ALSO A call to action. In keeping with that, I want to let everyone know that I am not content to be a thinker and writer about this topic. I am going to take part in bringing this vision into manifestation, and provide as much leadership as I can. To that end, I have recently founded a non-profit organization, the Center for Civil Economics. One of the most important goals of this NGO will be working out ways to achieve the tangible manifestation of one or more civil endowments. We will also conduct research and communications on the topic, and cooperate with others doing related work.

I hope I have adequately given credit in the text to sources of ideas I've found inspirational, such as the writings of Folkert Wilken, Peter Barnes, and many others. At the same time, I take full responsibility for this body of work. This is true for two reasons. The first is that it is a highly original set of ideas and proposals. It is not a derivative work. The second reason follows on the first, in the sense that if it is original, and if I am to claim responsibility for its good and creative qualities, I must also accept responsibility for any shortcomings as well. That is the proper thing to do when one puts forth an original system of ideas into the world—especially when it includes a proposal for tangible activity. And such action is urgently needed.

This human realm is deeply threatened in so many ways. Looking solely at the issue of climate change, it should be clear that we should not just be worried. We should be making fundamental changes, and not only in our personal behavior, but in our most fundamental systems.

One of the most important inspirations I've received from the Buddhist tradition is this: if we discover the true profundity of our humanity, our lives become incredibly precious. Extending this insight to the scale of the whole of human society, it becomes clear that doing whatever we can to create the conditions for the healthy flourishing of the human realm is the most compelling endeavor imaginable.

With that inspiration, and if you see the potential of the ideas in this book, I ask you to join with me in the work of creating a civil endowment system. It is a work with tremendous transformative potential for society—and for each of us engaged with it.

Whatever action you take going forward, I urge you to practice the six economic virtues of generosity, ethics, non-aggression, diligence, focus, and wisdom in your life. In doing so, you will be enacting your own authentic economics of compassion. The great work of our time—and the inspiration that sustains this vision of civil endowment—is the aspiration for a bright future for human civilization, one of unity, wellbeing, and fulfillment. May we each join in and do our part.

* * *

Acknowledgements

THIS BOOK EMBODIES CLOSE TO 20 YEARS OF RESEARCH and contemplation, and it would be impossible to cite all the people who have helped me, inspired me, and taught me in so many ways. But some strong themes stand out: My family members—my mother, Alice R. McCarthy, my father, the late Walter J. McCarthy Jr., his wife Linda McCarthy, and my siblings Walter, Sharon, James, and William and their families—have been incredibly consistent in their love and support over all this time. In my spiritual journey, the Ven. Khenpo Karthar Rinpoche, Ven. Bardor Tulku Rinpoche, the late Traleg Kyabgon Rinpoche, and Dzogchen Ponlop, Rinpoche—and other great Buddhist teachers— have shared their profound wisdom and blessings and given me incomparable personal guidance since the 1970s.

The fundamental idea of civil endowment came into focus for me over ten years ago, during periods of intensive study and contemplation that led me to "the leap." My friend Ilfra Halley was very much "present at the creation" during this period, and organized two informal discussions on the topic at her home. I am grateful to her and to other friends, including Judith Asphar and Deborah Bansemer, who understood the significance of the idea at that early stage.

It was not until 2009, however, that I made the first public presentation on civil endowment, which was given at Lifebridge Sanctuary in Rosendale, New York at the kind invitation of Barbara Valocore and Steve Nation. Around that time, I met Chris Hewitt as we were both becoming involved with the local currency project that has come to fruition as the Hudson Valley Current. Chris also asked me to start writing on economics for his newspaper,

Country Wisdom News. I am grateful for the confidence in me that he showed in giving me that opportunity. Chris also generously put his solid publication skills to work in the final preparation of this book.

I also offer my appreciation to my friends Carl Frankel and Sheri Winston, Rolan and Claudia, Andrea Hameed, Harvey Garrett, Jeff Davis, Mark Rothe, Peter and Brenda Swords, Michael and Margaret Erlewine, David Cagan, Bob Dandrew, Mary "Chiz" Chisholm, and all the members of the Money and Intuition group.

My lifelong friend Brad Ethington has been a consistent and supportive presence during the writing process. Brad's wife, Pamela Ethington, helped immensely in the late stages of production of the book by applying her excellent editorial skills to the final review of many of the chapters. My friend John Bloom deserves a special mention for his excellent, detailed feedback that greatly improved the clarity of chapters five and six.

Throughout the last several years, I have been privileged to enjoy regular, in-depth discussions with my dear friend and Dharma brother Jim Kukula on the subject matter of this book, and his support and insights have been tremendously valuable.

In the production of the book, I am thankful for the excellent professional work of Arya-francesca Jenkins (editing), Lisa Berry (graphics), Robert Hansen-Sturm (author photo), and Tilman Reitzle (book and cover design).

Finally, I would like to extend my special thanks to my longtime loved one, Carla Rodning. Her love and generosity have meant the world to me in this journey. Living with someone in the throes of a writing project is never easy, but her unconditional personal support—and excellent feedback—have been a tremendous source of strength.

Selected Bibliography

Alperovitz, Gar, and Lew Daly. *Unjust Deserts: How the Rich Are Taking Our Common Inheritance*. New York: New, 2008.

Barnes, Peter. *Capitalism 3.0: A Guide to Reclaiming the Commons*. San Francisco:Berrett-Koehler, Publishers Group West, 2006.

Barnes, Peter. *Who Owns the Sky?—Our Common Assets and the Future of Capitalism*. Washington, DC: Island Press, 2001.

Bollier, David, and Silke Helfrich. *The Wealth of the Commons: A World Beyond Market and State*. Amherst, MA: Levellers, 2012.

Bollier, David. *Think like a Commoner: A Short Introduction to the Life of the Commons*. New Society Publishers, 2014.

Boulding, Kenneth E. *The Economy of Love and Fear: a Preface to Grants Economics*. Belmont, CA: Wadsworth Pub., 1973.

Brown, Lester R. *The Great Transition*. New York: W. W. Norton & Co., 2015.

Daly, Herman E., John B. Cobb, and Clifford W. Cobb. *For the Common Good: Redirecting the Economy Toward Community, The Environment, and a Sustainable Future*. Boston: Beacon Press, 1994.

De Soto, Hernando. *The Mystery of Capital: Why Capitalism Triumphs in the West and Fails Everywhere Else*. New York: Basic Books, 2000.

Desaules, Marc, and Christopher Houghton. Budd. *A Human Response to Globalisation: Discovering Associative Economics*. Canterbury: Associative Economics Institute, 2003.

Flexner, Kurt F. *The Enlightened Society: The Economy with a Human Face*. Lexington Books, 1989.

Harvey, David. *The Enigma of Capital: And the Crises of Capitalism*. Oxford: Oxford University Press, 2011.

Hawken, Paul, Amory B. Lovins, and L. Hunter Lovins. *Natural Capitalism: Creating the Next Industrial Revolution*. Boston: Little, Brown, 1999.

Hawken, Paul. *Blessed Unrest: How the Largest Social Movement in History is Restoring Grace, Justice, and Beauty to the World*. New York: Penguin Books, 2008.

Hawley, James P., and Andrew T. Williams. *The Rise of Fiduciary Capitalism: How Institutional Investors Can Make Corporate America More Democratic.* Philadelphia: University of Pennsylvania, 2000.

Henderson, Hazel. *Creating Alternative Futures: The End of Economics.* West Hartford, CT: Kumarian Press, 1996.

His Holiness the Dalai Lama, and Laurens Van Den Muyzenberg. *The Leader's Way: The Art of Making the Right Decisions in Our Careers, Our Companies, and the World at Large.* New York: Broadway, 2009.

Korten, David C. *Agenda for a New Economy: From Phantom Wealth to Real Wealth.* 2nd ed. San Francisco: Berrett-Koehler, 2010.

Lux, Kenneth. *Adam Smith's Mistake: How a Moral Philosopher Invented Economics & Ended Morality.* Boston: Shambhala, 1990.

Macy, Joanna. *Mutual Causality in Buddhism and General Systems Theory: The Dharma of Natural Systems.* Albany: State U of New York, 1991.

McDonough, William, and Michael Braungart. *The Upcycle.* New York: North Point Press, a division of Farrar, Straus and Giroux, 2013.

Ostrom, Elinor. *Governing the Commons: The Evolution of Institutions for Collective Action.* New York: Cambridge University Press, 1990.

Piketty, Thomas. *Capital in the Twenty-first Century.* Trans. Arthur Goldhammer. Cambridge, MA: Harvard University Press, 2014.

Pribram, Karl. *A History of Economic Reasoning.* Baltimore: Johns Hopkins University Press, 1983.

Rinpoche, Bardor Tulku. *Living in Compassion.* 2nd ed. Kingston, NY: Rinchen Publications, 2004.

Schroyer, Trent. *Beyond Western Economics: Remembering Other Economic Cultures.* Abingdon, Oxon: Routledge, 2009.

Schumacher, E. F. *Small Is Beautiful: Economics as if People Mattered.* New York: HarperPerennial, 1989.

Schumpeter, Joseph A. *History of Economic Analysis.* New York: Oxford University Press, 1954.

Soros, George. *The Alchemy of Finance: Reading the Mind of the Market.* New York: Simon and Schuster, 1987.

Steiner, Rudolf, Gary Lamb, and Sarah Hearn. *Steinerian Economics: A Compendium.* Hillsdale, NY: Adonis Press, 2014.

Wilken, Folkert. *The Liberation of Capital.* London: Allen & Unwin, 1982.

DAVID NELSON McCARTHY (b. 1954) is an independent scholar, writer, and activist in the field of economics. He has been active in the sustainability movement, and is a co-founder of the Hudson Valley Current, a local currency system. He is the founder of Rinchen Publications and has been engaged with publishing Buddhist texts for over 25 years. He recently founded a new non-profit organization, The Center for Civil Economics (www.civil-economics.org), to conduct research, dialogue, and activism around civil society's role in the economy. He lives in Kingston, New York, and may be reached at civil.endowment@gmail.com.

Made in the USA
Middletown, DE
05 October 2015